Culturally On Plan

A Pragmatic Guide for Aligning
Organizational Culture with a Strategic Plan
and Transforming
~~Management~~→ to Leadership

Greg Lane

Also by Greg Lane

Made to Order Lean – Excelling in a High Mix, Low Volume Environment

Mr. Lean Buys and Transforms a Manufacturing Company –
The True Story of Profitably Growing an Organization with Lean Principles

Co-authored by Greg Lane

Toyota by Toyota – Reflections from the Inside Leaders on the Techniques That
Revolutionized the Industry

Culturally
On Plan

A Pragmatic Guide for Aligning
Organizational Culture with a Strategic Plan
and Transforming
~~Management~~→ to Leadership

Greg Lane

For my father's advise and devotion to editing and critiquing.
For the support and understanding of my wife Sonia and my daughters Sofia and Rebeca.

Table of Contents

Chapter 6: Analyzing Your Current Culture and Defining Your Desired Culture 79

Chapter 7: Analysis for the Cultural Transformation Plan 95

Chapter 10: Creating a Learning Environment   151

Chapter 11: Follow-up and Sustainment   159

Introduction

For many, instinct suggests an organization's culture influences the bottom line, though it's nearly impossible to quantify its financial impact. It's also challenging to lead change on these hazy (soft) issues. We often read about a company's crisis that led to new leadership which brought with it new traits and behaviors -- positively effecting the culture and ultimately improving profitability, but the chances of the current CEO and top leadership emulating another CEO's successful traits and behaviors is difficult. The CEO influences the organization's culture but does not necessary control it. The options are to continue supporting the organization's objectives with technical and market driven process improvements and only addressing 'soft' issues as necessary, or to enhance the technical actions by simultaneously engaging all the organization's leaders in examining the 'soft' skills that are required to maintain and continuously improve the technical solutions.

There are numerous studies and data that look to quantify the impact of cultural change, a representative study in 2012 including 50 global companies (which had maintained sufficient data) found the highly engaged organizations had nearly three times the operating margin of those with low engagement.[24] Additionally there is plenty of evidence confirming that process improvements are often not sustained when they are not accompanied by cultural change. Case studies, data and examples of what has successfully been utilized to lead a behavioral change are interwoven throughout the book.

I am a technical person and like many others find comfort in more technical process improvements, though after transforming my own organization and supporting many others, I have learned you need a simple and practical method that comprehensively addresses cultural change for sustainment and long-term profitability. The continuous improvement (or Lean) community has increased its focus on changing the culture with excellent methods like Gemba walks (the real place where value is created), exposing and resolving problems at their root cause and learning to become better coaches. Although these are all important parts of the technique shared, experience has shown a more comprehensive approach that engages and creates awareness improves the success rate.

So a practical method to lead cultural change that does not necessitate a top leadership shake-up is desirable. The keys to success are engagement followed by personal awareness. Ideally there is belief and drive for cultural change from the top, though pockets of success can also convince the CEO. The proven methodology being shared begins at the organizational (or plant) level by assessing the current culture and then determining the desired culture, but the real work takes place at the value stream and departmental (or positional) levels. Here it is demonstrated that working contrary to conventional wisdom obtains the best results, first the teams determine the desired behaviors to support the strategic objectives (the future state), and this engagement leads to simple methods of creating personal awareness of existing traits and behaviors (the current state) and then comparing those to the desired behaviors. With this in mind we must realize most of us are proven to be poor at assessing our own behaviors, but there are many simple, practical and non-biased ways to do this. So if we assume there is not a crisis (a burning platform), but instead challenging objectives to be met, we should utilize an approach that continuously develops our most valuable resource, our human assets.

Based on years of experimenting with cultural change, a few concepts that stand out as necessary considerations for successful cultural change are worth disclosing up-front. The *other guy* syndrome is predominant in human change. Most believe their success results from their traits and behaviors; therefore improving behaviors is something the *other guy* must do. The *other guy* maintains the same beliefs and waits for the '*other guy*', and so on, so without an organizational wide plan to develop non-biased self-awareness of your traits, you are only haphazardly creating random awareness which has little chance of success. Secondly, people don't resist change as much as they resist *BEING CHANGED,* so again engagement and awareness are key. And last is that people's mindset (that is, beliefs and values) has a profound influence on their decision-making. In this case, that influence applies to their working environment. These three considerations are all addressed in the techniques being shared.

At this point it is also worthwhile to define the implications of culture and why it affects the bottom line. The reference will always be toward the organization's culture, which can be defined as values, norms, habits and traits shared within a group, resulting in predicable behavior and having an influence on decision-making (in other words, "the way things get done here"). So if culture helps to improve decision-making, this is a point where we can begin quantifying what the wrong decisions have cost.

Before anyone can enthusiastically consider how to positively affect culture, you need to ensure the effort is justly rewarded. Therefore *Culturally On Plan* is exactly what the title infers, improving the culture to better support the strategic plan, this is demonstrated through examples of successful implementations. So to begin we need a clear strategic plan that is well *deployed* and supported throughout the organization. Experience shows that often the problem starts here, and CEO surveys confirm that although most have a strategy, its complete deployment throughout the company has rarely been accomplished through proper engagement.

Presumably you have a strategy, but even after your considerable effort and dedication in communicating your organization's priorities, you likely have only a few teammates who clearly understand and support your priorities in the manner in which you intended. You don't have to take my word for it. Instead, randomly sample five or ten associates from various levels and departments to see how they articulate and support the organization's goals, and what individual actions they've identified to support those targets. What you'll typically find is what you believed was clear in your team's mind is vague throughout the organization. An exception can be when you are reacting to a crisis, than it is likely that certain communications permeate the organization, though dealing with a crisis is outside the scope of this book.

People hear what you say, filter it through their *experiences, traits, and values*, and further judge its importance by how you demonstrate support through your actions. The situation is made worse if your actions don't support your words, or you or your top leaders are flavor-of-the-month types, who read a new book or hear a new idea, and immediately set out in a new direction.

Culturally On Plan begins by looking at why most organizations fail to maintain their process improvements. Then a practical method honed through experimentation within a number of organizations, aimed at aligning traits and behaviors with the strategic objectives, is shared. The method begins with better communicating and obtaining buy-in for the strategy with participative decision-making, but in a pragmatic and simple format. Remember not to overestimate the transparency of your goals or underestimate the importance of your team's diverse mentality when leading change. Following this a participative approach is introduced engaging leaders at all levels in defining the desired traits and behaviors necessary in meeting and exceeding the targets set forth in the annual strategy. Then comes a critical element of success, at the value stream level, defining the desired traits for each department and encouraging a private and non-biased self-awareness of the individual's behaviors.

After introducing many techniques to privately come to terms with your current traits and behaviors and how they affect decision-making in your working environment, the book explores practical and tangible actions that can be taken to alter behaviors and habits.

In addition to your personal awareness and gaining improvement ideas, this book will also help in your understanding of:

- The importance of the link between a properly deployed annual strategy and profitable cultural change.

- How current leadership can pragmatically engage and create awareness towards cultural change.

- Why a more comprehensive Cultural Transformation Plan is necessary in today's dynamic global environment and how to create this plan.

Many of us have shaped a successful career by implementing technical and market solutions and only dealing with the soft issues as necessary. Though if you are convinced that you shouldn't only formally focus on developing hard skills, but also have a practical and comprehensive plan how to improve the soft skills (increasing you human-capital), you are sure to come away with a framework and practical ideas. Additionally this will require awareness and techniques to deal with: intuitive versus analytical thinking, leading without power, creating a learning environment, which are all addressed in this book.

Having personally purchased and transformed a company that had 18 years of developed culture, along with 20+ years of supporting others in continuously improving, I hope by sharing my experiences on the fuzzy and often avoided 'soft' issues, it permits you to come away with a more comprehensive process to link a cultural plan with your strategic objectives.

This book is also meant to be a dynamic and learning tool, meaning it will be revised as new learnings (via experimentation) expose additional knowledge of cultural change. You are encouraged to share both successful and unsuccessful experiments that could be included in future editions. Please email me at glane@Strategic-Leaders.com with any experiences or comments worth sharing.

Note: There is a glossary of terms included in Appendix A that define terminology with which you are likely unfamiliar.

CHAPTER 1

Most Fail

Imagine you want to implement breakthrough objectives and realize to accomplish this you need to change some traits, habits and behaviors in the organization. First let's understand why others are unsuccessful in this endeavor.

Why Lean Fails

Two-thirds of lean (continuous improvement) implementations result in failure ("failure" being defined as not having attained sustainable results by creating a lean culture), while only about 16 percent of the ones studied achieved sustained results.[1] That is quite a statistic to open with, especially if you're a proponent of lean. But I believe it's best to start with the cold, hard facts and work our way toward understanding why this happens and what has been demonstrated in helping to overcome this high failure rate.

Let's first consider some of the reasons transformations fail. Again, failure in this respect equates to not attaining sustainable results with a continuous improvement culture being ingrained into the organization. Another way to think about the problem is that the soft skills have not progressed in sync with the hard skills. Organizational culture is important for many reasons ("culture" meaning the values, norms, and traits shared within a group, resulting in predicable behavior and having an influence on decision-making), although a principle focus in this book is its influence on decision-making, as that can have profound effects on profit.

Following the reasons for failures, I will present a methodology that can be consolidated into a simple visual, but it is based on individual awareness of behaviors helping to identify many of the soft issues that are often overlooked. This has realigned successful cultural changes by increasing their awareness and avoiding the pitfalls. The underlying work in creating the two matrices shown in the illustration (Figure 2.1) will prove challenging, although as most know, the real challenge is the altering of the traits and behaviors required for the new culture. A more detailed discussion will follow that helps identify (person by person within the organization) which characteristics will likely *not* align with a successful cultural change and some ideas that have helped overcome these shortfalls.

In this chapter, you'll consider whether some, all, or a combination of the reasons for failure are present in you organization. The better you can articulate which issues apply, the easier it will be to consider how the proposed solutions can be successful and how best to gain cultural acceptance.

Note: Throughout the book, when speaking of a "lean transformation" or a "cultural change," I am referring to the same thing, as lean is all about cultural change.

Is Leadership Responsible for Success?

Let's consider how culture and leadership account for an organization's success by considering the following definition of success.

- success = ability + luck

Now think of all the businesses you have come across that appear to have little or no ability and instead lots of luck. The right location, started at the right time, no real competition, representing a great product although they may have terrible salesmanship, and so on. Now consider either of these two definitions:

- very successful = lots of ability + some luck

- very successful = some ability + lots of luck

This is a critical point to consider as we search to rationalize the world around us, and specifically success in business. Often stories are presented to try and explain business success through various avenues, most predominate are the leadership traits, and these stories, books, or movies usually give undeserved and excessive credit to the leadership and discount or ignore the factor of luck. What can you say or write about luck, by its definition (favoring chance) it is outside our influence of control. It sells more books to those searching to rationalize and copy success, to believe success can be completely controlled. On the other hand to concede that an individual or organization's success was based heavily on luck will likely be a shorter story and sell fewer books to those searching to understand and control the world around them. If you think about luck in business, it is not really defined so much by what the organization does, but instead what the market or competitors do or don't do. What transpires in the market and with the competition is what has the most dramatic effect on your luck or lack thereof.

Let's look at some data for a moment that supports the theory that what is published as successful does not always account for the true underlying factors and likely luck comes and goes but lends a determining hand in the final outcome. A 2008 study reviewed *Fortune* magazine's list of America's Most Admired Companies for the 23-year period from 1983 to 2006 and concluded that the returns on "stocks of the admired companies had lower returns on average, than stocks of despised companies" during this period.[2] Attributes of admired companies usually include superior leadership, excellent cultures, technological or market leaders, and so on. The study goes on to conclude that the effect of admired companies is positive but is paid for in lower returns and these returns varied from year to year. It's likely luck also played a factor on and off for some of these companies, but it's hard to factor this in. Remember luck in business is strongly effected by outside forces like the market and the actions (or lack of) from your competitors.

Just for thought, consider companies like Facebook and Google. Although many of the stories written look at the founders, as well as the developments and actions that led to their great successes, consider what their fates would have been like without any luck. A timely topic is also Apple Computer; it would be hard to argue that they haven't created great products and deserve considerable success. Redefining how we use a telephone or a personal digital assistant are great accomplishments requiring unprecedented abilities, but also consider how luck played its part; for example, no other company stumbled upon, developed, or successfully marketed better products during the same period.

Therefore, I don't want to discount luck and the critical role it plays, and I am not attempting to write another book on leadership and cultural change that tries only to correlate leadership and cultural change to success. Because luck is affected by chance, there is little to be said except "good luck;" instead, I want to focus on some of the factors I have observed that led to unsuccessful culture changes and offer a simple method that, if really focused on over a period of time, will reduce many of the failure factors. Luck is only a consideration in this book because it is an important distinction when reviewing your past decisions and working your way toward improving your own decision-making process. In Chapter 8, we will discuss the importance of understanding how you make decisions and tracking your hypotheses against their results. And, periodically, luck plays its hand. We want to make sure this does not create false expectations or biases in our future decision-making.

We are often mesmerized by stories that link a few personal traits or strategies with great success. We immediately want to copy or emulate these even if they are an illusion. It is like buying this book and believing that strategy deployment and the Cultural Transformation Plan alone will lead to a successful cultural transformation, when it will likely also require years of dedication, hard work, and possibly a little luck along the way.

Defining a Successful Lean Transformation

Before considering why lean transformations might be considered a failure, it might be best to first define what we mean by a successful one. Common definitions of lean thinking (not lean manufacturing) would include some of the following:

- Maximizing customer value by continuously reducing waste

- Optimizing complete flow across value streams

- Leading either a product or service enterprise to continuously improve quality, productivity, and effectiveness.

- Creating a no blame culture where people are encouraged to identify and evoke problems as a method to learn and improve.

- Developing engaged people (human-capital acquisition) by focusing on soft skills.

Naturally, the ultimate result of implementing lean thinking should result in improved earnings (generally EBIT, Earnings Before Interest and Taxes, can be utilized). Although lean thinking suggests by focusing on the non-financial numbers, which have a direct correlation to the financials in your strategy deployment, everyone can be engaged in achieving the best long term financial results.

On the other hand, more narrow thinking limits the potential and expectations when we only talk about lean manufacturing. This is a point of contention when I hear people use this terminology because the minute you follow the word "lean" with "manufacturing," you have limited yourself to a tools approach and narrowed down your expectations to just the operations team (assuming you are a manufacturer). Naturally this also limits the potential audience outside the manufacturing sector; therefore, some organizations avoid this pitfall by instead using words like "continuous improvement" to guide their transformation.

A successful lean transformation is creating a sustainable cultural that would likely include some of the following concepts: internal discipline, new norms, acceptance of change, small but continuous improvement, innovative and adaptive, continuously challenging, and effective communication.

It becomes overwhelming to think of developing all the previous concepts throughout most corporate cultures but fear not, the problem of change is not as difficult as commonly perceived. Toyota estimates two to four percent of an organization's team are innovative and adaptive individuals willing to push ideas, while only up to four percent are blockers who go out of their way to block and resist change. Everyone else is sitting on the fence waiting to see which way the wind blows. Think where you want to spend your time, pushing the blockers to transform or supporting the change agents?

Reasons for Lean Failures

In this section, I share what I have experienced as the reasons organizations fail to achieve sustainable cultural change. Common in almost all reasons for failure is that something is being imposed without having everyone involved, and not having a PDCA cycle (Plan Do Check Act – scientific method) allowing the ability to learn and adapt in today's dynamic environment. The eleven reasons mentioned are not inclusive but are the most common. I have listed them roughly in order of occurrence.

Taking a Tools Approach

Choosing a team who then select a few lean tools to take into the organization in search of problems where the tools can be applied is basically a form of *kamikaze kaizen* (suicidal continuous improvement) and has about the same probability of long term success as winning the lottery. Years ago, the lean community identified the shortcomings of the tools approach when implementing lean, so it's not surprising it is the most common reason mentioned for failures. The difficulty is in finding the balance between just implementing tools and tackling the culture and soft issues that have to be overcome. Let's face it: the tools approach is appealing, because

- It can be shuffled off to others.

- It is almost sure to get some short-term benefits. Tools like 5S (workplace organization), standardized work, changeover time reductions, and the like are sure to generate one-off savings and likely to also result in some annual savings.

- It's tangible, and the tools are simple to understand, technically.

- It can be done and implemented rather quickly.

- If it fades over time, the big boss can often save face as he or she did not personally have ownership or responsibility.

Methods/tools like standardized work for managers or A3 Problem Solving (problem resolution on a single 11×17 piece of paper) instill a discipline in the follow-up and create a culture change, they are often prescribed at some point during a transformation. I, myself, am a strong proponent of management standardized work and A3 Problem Solving and have observed their considerable benefits, but I have also learned that they must be combined with a deeper understanding of human nature, namely our inherent comfort level in taking the easy road and reverting to old methods. "Why not revert to the old ways?" the thinking goes, "when they have been successful in the past, it's likely the new method isn't receiving the follow through it should, and it has probably not yet been fully proved out." But each time you allow someone to revert back, you reinforce the old methodology.

So implementing tools is not wrong and is a critical part of every lean transformation that I have been involved with. Whether tools should come first or leadership and culture issues should take precedence is a question that could likely be debated into the next decade. Many will say that a few successful lean tools, which have short-term quantifiable results, will help sell lean within the organization. Others who are well along their lean journeys started with awareness, training, and then implemented tools, and who is to say that's not right? Instead of spending effort trying to establish a recipe, the focus here is to offer an enhanced approach, no matter where you find yourself on the journey.

We can learn from a historical example of which many of us are unaware, a strong influence of Toyota's methodologies came from Training Within Industry (TWI), a U.S. program developed during World War II to ramp up production of badly needed war supplies. Although the principals and tools were based on the earlier work of Charles Allen, they predominately focused on "the needs of supervisors."[3] Early on there was a clear recognition between successful productivity improvements and the supervisors' possessing the skills to instruct and develop human relations. After studying TWI's results, Toyota also recognized this link to enhance productivity and made it a foundation of their leadership. So although first recognized centuries before, *job relations* was reinforced (as TWI data demonstrates) as a critical counterpart to the *improvement tools*—back in the 1940s!

Lack of Consistency in Purpose without Strategy Deployment

"Flavor of the month" is a phrase that comes to mind. People read articles or books, attend a seminar, further their education, or someone new enters the organization, and you now have new ideas to implement. Naturally this is something you want, a dynamic and learning organization, but you must ensure this does not come at the price of jumping on every new fad or idea that comes along. Doing so leads to failed transformations, as it leaves people confused, insecure, not participating, and preoccupied with what direction they will be pushed in.

Strategy deployment, combined with good leadership, will ensure this does not happen. Everything you do in terms of cultural change and continuous improvement should have a clear link, a golden thread (linking actions to the strategic objectives they support) visualized throughout the organization's structure, including objectives that connect one level of priorities to the company's priorities. Strategy deployment further advocates a few critical objectives instead of many objectives that will dilute your focus and energy (and rarely will an organization have the resources to execute an annual plan that has more than five or six key goals). A connection that clarifies how a particular action or indicator helps attain our primary objectives is a key responsibility of the leadership team. If that golden thread has not been communicated and clarified, then a new idea or methodology is likely to start with fireworks and end in a fizzle.

The media, our national structure, and your organization's culture offer a big reward to those who resolve crises. Look at publications that rank our corporate and public leaders, and you'll find that those at the top have averted a crisis within the organization or have resolved a disaster for the public's benefit, and this has led to recognition and promotion. We need to ensure in a cultural change that our leaders have patience and realize that, as well as saving the day or firefighting for quick results, it is just as important to have small but continuous improvements that are supported and rewarded regularly within the organization's culture.

True *continuous improvement* is a cultural change that requires a belief, patience, and a long-term commitment, even as most corporate cultures demand demonstrating success in a short period. The CEO's longevity, the company's stock prices, the patience of the board of directors are all considerations in large publically traded companies, so we focus much less on *Fortune* 500 companies in this book and much more on making these transformations successful for small and medium enterprises (or SMEs). This is not to say that SMEs are immune to the importance of speed, and when the methods presented here are combined with some short-term results from implementing tools, results will follow quickly.

Many companies start on a lean journey with the sense that this is something *additional,* or begin changing the culture because someone new has come on board and has determined the need for change. But not showing the link between these activities and the organization's objectives is a big mistake and creates a lack of consistency. Although many lean proponents have a strategy, the discussion in this book may lead you to realize that you do not yet have it deployed throughout the organization, where all levels of leadership have a chance to contribute and buy-in. This is the way that cultural change begins.

Missing the Cultural Transformation Plan

Of the failed transformations I have come across, not considering how to transform the existing cultural and mentality is likely the most serious shortcoming; therefore, connecting a cultural transformation with strategic objectives is the focus of this book. Reaching the strategic objectives often requires not only focusing on actions and improving hard skills, but sustainment relies on improving the soft skills. It is introduced here only for you to contemplate this shortcoming in your organization, while details of a Cultural Transformation Plan are introduced in Chapter 5.

Openly admitting that your organization requires a change in culture is by itself a big step. Ideally, a Cultural Transformation Plan is done on a personal level by evaluating each person's traits and behaviors and comparing those to the desired traits and behaviors in the new culture. In this case *cultural* (really referring to the organizational culture, is defined as the values, traits, and behaviors that constitute the uniqueness of the environment and affect its decision-making) will also include philosophies, experiences, psychology, and attitudes. Obviously this opens a can of worms, but without such a plan, your lean transformation will not create a sustainable culture change, and you will struggle in reaching your strategic objectives.

I propose this Cultural Transformation Plan be considered for each individual from top management through the first line supervision (at least), with consideration given to including team leaders. When defining what I mean by this and how you might go about it, I am making the assumption that the people within your team for whom this applies have the aptitude and abilities that you require and understand that a cultural change involves everybody. So I am talking about having a unique plan for each person in a leadership role, although many elements in these plans could be common.

An assumption in making a Cultural Transformation Plan for each individual in the leadership team is that each is willing to invest effort into changing for the good of the organization. A quote I've picked up along the way that might clarify what I am getting at is,

"You need to change the person or you need to CHANGE THE PERSON." If you follow the meaning, we will assume that either team members can be convinced and will apply effort toward altering their styles to contribute in the newly defined culture, or you will take the appropriate actions to move them into positions that are less critical in respect to the required cultural change. (Or they are removed from the organization.) In Chapter 5, you'll be introduced to what is meant by a Cultural Transformation Plan and how this plan can keep you focused, and thus overcome many of reasons for failures cited within this chapter.

The first step in moving toward a Cultural Transformation Plan is analyzing your organization's existing culture. This is often overlooked, but you must first understand why you have the culture you do, before you can define where you want to go. An organization's culture develops to help it cope with its environment; therefore, you must understand what is changing in the environment that requires the culture to change, and then clearly communicate this. Often this requires analysis, which is something humans avoid if we can instead intuitively create a solution. By performing an analysis to define your existing culture and why you have it, you will better understand your requirements for moving toward a new culture.

Not Changing the Metrics and Expectations

Another critical reason transformations fail to become sustainable is from not using the correct measurements, or from not setting continuously improving targets. Without setting the correct continuously moving expectations, and instead treating a transformation as a project or program with one-time targets, you will not be challenging and advancing the team. In other words, the error is that those in touch with the process do not continuously revise the expectations.

I am *not* referring to intuitively setting goals without actually observing the process and its problems, as can happen with managers and directors. Instead, you want leaders who, through close involvement in continuous improvement, identify waste and are involved in determining improvement actions. They have the ingrained belief that the process can always be improved, so they set realistic expectations (likely leading to new norms) within the organizational culture. By contrast, more traditional management might start a project with certain metrics and objectives and set very aggressive goals within a short time frame, but once the project has ended, no ongoing improvement is targeted or monitored, and no new expectations are set.

Also important is utilizing the right metrics, also known as KPIs (key performance indicators), and measurements, which should also incorporate *leading indicators.* The famous quotations of "What gets measured, gets improved" and "If you don't measure it, it doesn't improve" come to mind. To use the right measures, start with good strategy deployment (which could also be called policy deployment if that didn't sound like bureaucratically rolling out policies), and as it is being deployed through the various levels you need to ensure the metrics are aligned. Limit the metrics assigned to any one person to four or five, as it has been demonstrated that humans lose focus and perspective when any individual is assigned more than this. In supporting your metrics, you might have some leading indicators (single process gauges that change well in advance of the underlying trend) that others can focus on in real time to move the metric in right direction. In Chapter 3 the difference between metrics and indicators will be better clarified.

Remember that just creating new or additional metrics will likely highlight more problems, thereby overloading team members and driving them to return to their old firefighting methods (that, in their minds, have worked so well in the past). Therefore, your metrics need to be well thought out and tied to the correct support structure.

Managing Rather than Leading

Leading is about respecting people, which brings out the best in everyone, while managing focuses on communicating decisions and demanding results. This is easy to define but changing from a manager to a leader is no simple task. Leadership is associated more with the core of someone's personality than management is. Does that mean you have to be born with the traits of a leader? No. But you do have to be willing to learn.

On the other hand, managers are trained in what is considered by some an art, and by others a science. Management is often referred to as a process to drive improvements in skills, know-how, and attitudes. Although parts of the respective definitions of managing and leading contain similar words like creating visions, coordinating, and accomplishing objectives, *leadership* has a distinct vocabulary, including sharing visions, balancing interests, creative, coaching, mentoring, and team members. *Management,* on the other hand, encompasses words like planning, organizing, directing, and controlling, and refers to the team as "employees."

Most importantly an underlying cause of these failures is that management is more in the direction of a "push" system and leadership is more a "pull" system. This is reinforced by the titles of the people involved in management; for example, if you have *directors* (which already sends an interesting message as the connotation of directing is an action of pushing, usually downward) directing *employees* (not team members), you are already setting a management tone, not a leadership tone. So this distinction starts even with our job titles, is driven from childhood, and is reinforced in business school.

To avoid failure, focus on moving toward leadership, which is a pull system with engaged team members instead of employees. Becoming more of a coach and mentor and balancing the conflicting interests of stakeholders to meet the organization's goals is no easy task, but those traits can be learned. The first steps involve awareness and self-reflection, but by the fact you are reading this book and can share it with others, your awareness level has already increased, and you'll begin formulating an action plan for moving toward leadership and growing an organization of future leaders. Doing so means a critical difference between a sustainable transformation and one that never realizes its potential.

Two other traits required for good leadership are courage and humility, which are not prevalent in most management approaches. Courage could be defined as having the guts to experiment with your own new ideas—even though there is a probability they will fail and you could lose face. In a lean culture, you want brainstorming and new ideas, and you want to use the PDCA method (also known as hypothesis, trial, verify hypothesis, roll-out), but you need leaders to demonstrate that it's okay to take risks, and that failures should be learned from and a natural part of a learning organization.

Humble leadership can be accomplished by admitting you do not know everything or have all of the answers. This can even be expressed when problem solving; for example, leaders should feel comfortable asking their team how to perform an analysis of higher-level data that would typically have been considered the territory of top leaders. A leader not only needs to demonstrate his or her human side, but also needs to expose *all* the problems in the organization, and needs to do this by questioning/listening instead of telling.

An important link to the earlier discussion on success = ability + luck is that leadership is often given undue and excessive credit for success in many contemporary publications, and luck is overlooked. Being humble allows you to recognize the part that luck plays. And then you can categorize which elements of past successes were due to luck, as opposed to leadership traits, and then focus on how those traits can be expanded for future successes.

Some are of the school of thought that leaders are born, and managers can be trained. I am of the opinion that you can learn to be a better leader by recognizing the value of people. This book will proceed on two assumptions: 1) some people can learn to be better leaders, and 2) an organization can become more successful by improving some leadership skills but not necessarily transforming all managers into leaders, leaving some combination of leaders and managers. You can then go forward, utilizing the best skills where appropriate.

Leadership Not Understanding the Commitment

The daily effort required in leading a cultural change can be imagined, but is not easy to completely grasp its difficulty until you are there. Having led my own change and supported others during the process, I have a great deal of respect for the commitment involved, although I often fail to see it displayed. With cultural change, the leader may understand that he or she will play a key role, but likely doesn't understand the need to change some of his or her own behaviors and traits. Cultural change cannot be managed like a project, and to that end, the practical method discussed in this book highlights in the planning phase what leadership behaviors will likely require change. Serious consideration must be given to the feasibility of making such changes.

The best advice is for you or your CEO to meet with a CEO of an organization that's a similar size and type, and that has successfully led a cultural transformation. You will get a chance to understand the personal experiences and learnings from leading this cultural change. If you can't find a similar situation, try the next best thing: reading, attending conferences, and speaking to people with transformation experiences. Although it's critical for the CEO to understand the tools, most important is to concentrate on leading the soft issues of cultural change by personally demonstrating the desired traits and behaviors.

Here again, it is important to note that I am specifically using the word "leadership," which is quite different then management. Management is a push style and is top-down, where leadership is more a pull and associated with equality, in which everyone is motivated by a better understanding of his or her objectives in relation to the organizational goals. A strong part of the transformation is moving from management toward leadership.

Not Creating a New Support Structure

A typical approach that has not been shown to sustain long-term improvement involves delegating the implementation of the transformation to someone (other than the CEO) and not changing the organizational structure to support this. That is, just piling on more work without removing any responsibilities.

By delegating, I mean assigning a *lean* or *continuous improvement champion* to implement the program with periodic reviews by management. (I hope you already recognize some of the problems with the language and connotation of words like "implement" and "management," which give the impression of pushing a project and directing an implementation.) There is absolutely nothing wrong with designating some trained and engaged individuals to support the transformation, even as full time resources. But the leader of a transformation must be from the top tier of the organization and focus on cultural change and on identifying where the current structure cannot support all the new demands being placed on individuals, reassigning responsibilities, as appropriate.

When referring to a new support structure, I am not suggesting that more people are required. I am suggesting that clearer definitions of responsibilities are necessary. After years of working with Toyota and two decades of supporting transformations, one continuing trend is the confusion of roles and responsibilities in reference to problem solving. Most organizations unknowingly and unwittingly place the responsibility of problem solving spread across all the organization's members, who may be untrained in resolving problems. In fact, I continuously observe shop floors and offices where workers deal with their own problems (many of which they have come to accept as normal and unconsciously utilize workarounds as part of their daily routines). This leads to unconsciously accepting about a 75–80 percent effectiveness of process times in most areas of the business.

Let's take a simple production situation: a worker has a problem with an electronic screw driver, she fumbles with it for a couple of minutes, and finally makes the decision that she cannot fix it and goes walking about looking for help. Imagine the cost to the organization (lost time fumbling, looking for help, never resolving the root cause), but in reality the time is factored in because we live with it each day and somehow still meet customer demand.

But let's compare this to the Toyota system. They load the operators closer to 95 percent occupancy (or effectiveness) and move problem resolution to team leaders as part of the support structure. This means there is no time allowed for resolving problems during normal production, so team members are given a quick communication method (without stopping their work or leaving the work station) called an *Andon* (an audio and visual alert sounded for an immediate response) to quickly receive help. In this case, the operator's only responsibility is to communicate the problem to the team leader and move on to the next job (as she is 95 percent loaded, she has no allowable time to resolve the issue) and the team leader resolves the issue and completes the work on that unit. Remember that financing the team leader comes from the difference between Toyota's 95 percent load on the operators and the 75 percent load I observe in other companies. This 20 percent difference pays for 1 team leader for approximately every 5 team members. A misconception in some explanations of the Toyota system is that everyone resolves problems, actually everyone can identify problems and improvement opportunities (through participative suggestion systems, and the like) and frequently can help resolve them outside production time. But within Toyota's manufacturing environment, team leaders have special training and specific responsibilities to resolve problems (at their root cause, when possible). This is only one example of how we must think through the support structure as part of a transformation, not necessarily adding additional headcount, but demonstrating clearly defined responsibilities for both the team member and the team leader.

One final note in regard to the support structure within Toyota's approach: they also have a central group of full time specialists to support their continuous improvement. During my training in Japan in the early 1990s, the English equivalent name for this group was OMCD (Operations Management Consulting Division) and at the time I believe there were about 20 or more in this group in Toyota City to support nine assembly plants. The important distinction is these groups of experts were not the process leaders; they were a support group with expertise brought in to facilitate various initiatives identified by the operational or departmental leadership.

Confusion Between Implementing Lean and Maintaining Existing Expectations

Another cause of unsuccessful transformations is the confusion of priorities between implementing a new culture and keeping day-to-day business operating. This follows on from three of the previously mentioned reasons for failure: not changing the metrics and expectations, not creating a new support structure, and managing instead of leading. In this case, it is a bit of "And on top of everything else, you want me to implement lean." Unless the burning platform is pure survival, whatever has led to past success is expected to continue, while the continuous improvement (and cultural change) are thought to be something additional that will lead to a bit more profitability. If you do not use lean metrics (for example, measuring *effectiveness* instead of *efficiency*), and do not continuously set new expectations, you will look at this as a project to work on when you have time available—in-between the day-to-day firefighting.

The same follows if the roles and responsibilities are not reviewed and updated: human nature will revert to the daily tried and true routines. Leadership, along with strategy deployment, are the keys to recognizing this and shifting away from survival to a real focus on strategic objectives, like profitability and growth. This further lends itself to the recommended structure offered in this book, which considers an improved strategy deployment that might entail discarding some measurements and replacing them with new, more encompassing ones. The metrics being discarded must be clearly communicated, but if the strategy deployment process is properly led, this will be part of the two-way discussions as the strategy is deployed through each subsequent layer in the organization.

Not Creating Stakeholder Consequences

The lack of stakeholder consequences resulting in failed transformations is similar to other causes of failure, with slight distinctions. An ideal approach would be that, if the CEO were the leader of the cultural change, he or she would be the driving force, find the time to be first for training and awareness, and then follow up with a train-the-trainer approach. Since this is not always the case, we want our strategy as simple and transparent as possible to help overcome a less-than-ideal approach.

The CEO may also lead the transformation and commit to some up-front training, but may not be the detailed implementer of the tools; instead others will be identified and trained as experts. In this case, you want the focus of top leadership's initial training to be on defining the new culture more so than with the continuous elimination of waste. In other words, the CEO needs to incorporate those traits and behaviors that are required to create a lean culture instead of thinking only in terms of lean manufacturing. If the CEO gets his mind around this cultural change and some of the other reasons previously mentioned for failures (for example, the necessity of a new support structure, or new measurements, or leadership instead of managing), you are already far in front of the two-thirds that have failed. Remember if you are a small- to medium-sized enterprise (SME), many of these cultural issues are difficult but are more surmountable than in a large *Fortune* 500 multinational.

The Cultural Transformation Plan that is recommended in this book is a system for creating stakeholder consequences throughout all leadership levels. In the planning stage, by utilizing self-assessments, each leader determines any traits or behaviors requiring realignment to meet the desired cultures requirements. Then those leaders must assess the reality of changing their behaviors, and if they feel confident in being able to achieve this, they can go into planning some tangible actions.

Distrust

If there is distrust with the leadership, a lack of confidence in their abilities, or a lack of respect, the company's existing culture will naturally resist a transformation. Typically consultants and advisors recommend that leaders publically commit to nobody losing their jobs due to improvements. This is critical, but even more important is having a hands-on leadership approach. Start with a clear strategy deployed through each level of the organization and a link (the golden thread, if you will) of how lean will support attaining these strategic objectives; follow this with support and checking-up, which are critical in sustaining these public statements. No one losing their jobs due to improvements is usually an easy commitment, especially if you have objectives for growth or a high attrition rate. But demonstrating real leadership, including coaching and mentoring, validates much more of a commitment to the team and will go a long way toward dissolving any distrust.

Dave LaHote, a colleague at the Lean Enterprise Institute said, "Senior managers overestimate their effectiveness, particularly as they seek to improve their organizations through formal initiatives. And they underestimate the impact (often negative) of their daily personal actions on employees." In other words, it's not what you say, but what you do. If you believe this statement, then you can imagine that daily leadership including coaching and mentoring the team to develop and advance themselves is more important than publically making the job loss statement (assuming it is followed through on). Building trust is about respecting people and the role they perform for the company, and that is what good leaders do.

Cookie Cutter Approach Leads to Unsuccessful Transformations

The cookie cutter approach can be viewed more in terms of utilizing lean manufacturing or a tools approach in trying to standardize continuous improvement steps across the organization's processes, departments, and divisions. Standardization is a critical lean element as it is necessary as a baseline from which you can improve a process. But trying to standardize lean implementation across various types of processes that experience vastly different problems is likely to fail. Many would agree that 5S (workplace organization) is a good place to start, and this can be followed by standardized work, but what if the process is not stable enough for standardization? The larger problem is trying to use textbook examples from the automotive industry and push those across all departments or into high variation businesses (and/or into transactional processes) and assume a similar approach will work throughout your organization.

Having specialized for many years at helping SMEs, made-to-order, and job-shop businesses implement lean cultures, I have often encountered organizations that began their transformations trying a cookie cutter approach. Either someone within the organization studied and trained on a tool, or a consultant experienced in high volume lean principals entered an organization and tried to sell a packaged approach. For example, this could manifest itself by attempting to force takt time or kanban (that is, a replenishment scheduling system helping to determine what, when, and how much to produce based on replenishment) into every process, without considering if the tool is necessary and solves a problem. Normally you need to revert to the lean principal the particular tool is trying to achieve, and then ask if the principal can be achieved in another way, say, with modifying the tool or using another approach. You also need to consider whether the improvement of that particular process will benefit from that principal or tool instead of blindly developing a rollout schedule just because the methodology was beneficial for another area.

Let's take the example of takt time, attempting to implement this as a tool across the entire organization. We could say that a first step would be to calculate takt time for the organization, and then, if necessary, calculate it for the various processes.

takt time = time available/customer demand

Imagine trying this in a job-shop. It would be difficult to calculate because they are selling their available time to distinct customers for a variety of products; therefore, time available varies each day depending on other sales and scheduling. Customer demand (the denominator in takt time) also continuously varies depending on daily demand.

Do not try the cookie cutter approach, but go back to lean principles, in this case the principal is to understand your customer's demand in relation to available time (so it can be compared to capacity). For a job-shop, customer demand is best defined in the job estimate (job costing) where time and materials were specified. The estimated time can instead be utilized in the planning and replace the takt time. This can be accomplished visually in real time by visually scheduling with a tool called a day-by-the-hour board. Even this visual schedule might require different formats for distinct processes and might not be applicable for every process. This is a simple example where a cookie cutter approach is a lazy and misapplied method, usually resulting in frustration and undermining faith in lean implementations.

The other extreme is creating hidden pockets of lean implementation spread throughout the organization, which is not a desirable result either. The most important aspect is not to have a bit of training here and a bit of implementation there, as this is typically not clarified with the team or linked to the overall strategy, and will only cause disillusioned team members to lose faith in leadership and lean.

Summary

Although this chapter might appear pessimistic by summarizing some common reasons for failures within cultural changes, I imagine there are readers well into lean journeys who can relate with some of these issues. The critical point from this discussion is to better quantify the root causes of why your transformation might not be attaining sustainable results. Summarizing the possible reasons for failure within cultural transformations:

- Tools approach

- Lack of consistency in purpose without strategy deployment

- Missing a cultural transformation plan

- Not changing the metrics and expectations

- Managing instead of leading

- Top leadership not understanding the commitment

- Not creating a new support structure

- Confusion between implementing lean and maintaining existing expectations

- Not creating stakeholder consequences

- Distrust

- Cookie cutter approach

This is by no means a complete list but the more you recognize where you fit in, the better you will be able to articulate the root causes and address some of the proposed ideas to resolve them.

Throughout this book, the three issues I will focus on are:

- Lack of consistency in purpose without strategy deployment

- Missing a cultural transformation plan

- Managing instead of leading

I choose these because the proven method in this book focuses on these three areas, and then indirectly addresses most of the other causes of failure mentioned here. Using this top-three approach will keep the process simpler (in a relative sense) and allow you to better visualize how to minimize these pitfalls that will derail your journey and cultural improvement.

The methodology presented involves a high level of engagement to improve behaviors leading to sustainability of process improvements. A large survey, involving more than 32,000 people in 29 markets worldwide, demonstrates a 27.4% operating margin for 'high sustainable engagement companies' versus a 9.9% operating margin for 'low traditional engagement companies'.[24] So there is evidence to link engagement in changing behaviors with higher margins.

I start the next chapter with a quick overview of how strategy deployment links with the Cultural Transformation Plan. Then I present an overview of how important a well-deployed strategy is to sustained improvement and why this should be developed and visualized in the form of a matrix.

CHAPTER 2

Properly Deploying Your Strategy

There are no magical or quick processes to circumvent the reasons for failing to reach your breakthrough targets, although you can find many similarities in the steps taken by the successful frontrunners in aligning their human assets.

Steps to Cultural Transformation

A cultural transformation to address the soft issues for developing people's capabilities requires lots of determination, hard work, and involvement, although the common thread in attaining success can be divided in two parts:

1. Properly deploying the strategic objectives

2. Evolving a Cultural Transformation Plan

    *   Assessing the desired traits and behaviors vital in supporting the strategy

    *   Creating awareness of leadership's current traits and behaviors

    *   Identifying opportunities and actions to align differences between the desired and current behaviors (i.e. the culture)

A simplified way to visualize and summarize these two steps is displayed by the computer-generated image (Figure 2.1). You are not just creating matrices to add to your organization's existing pile; instead, by looking at the photo (Figure 2.2) of the dynamic and flexible white paper and Post-it Note process, you can imagine the interaction and dialogue taking place. Each cell (Post-it) is a combination of shared information, dialogue, increased awareness, awakenings, relations, and new trust being developed. Imagine, for example, the discoveries as each department systematically questions whether they have *control* or *influence* over each objective.

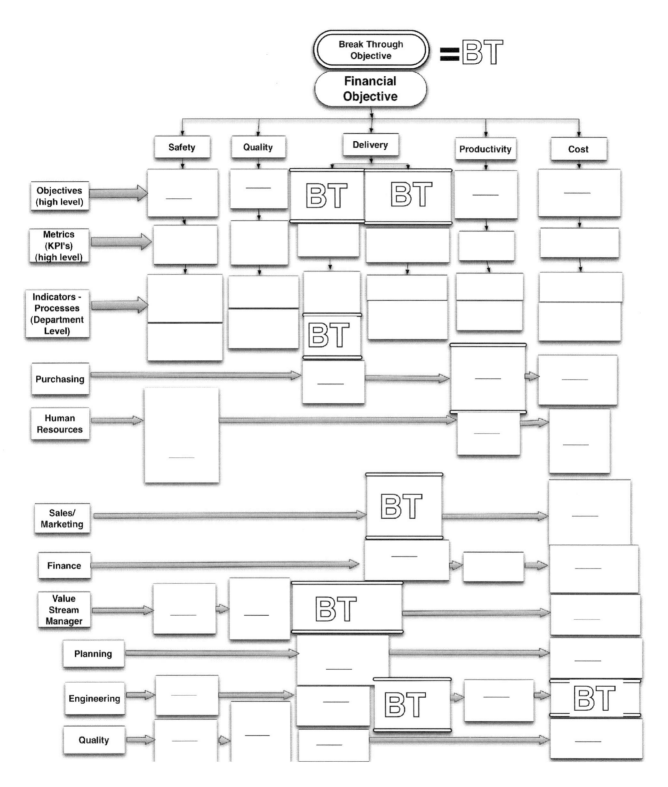

Figure 2.1 Strategy Deployment Matrix (annual at plant level)

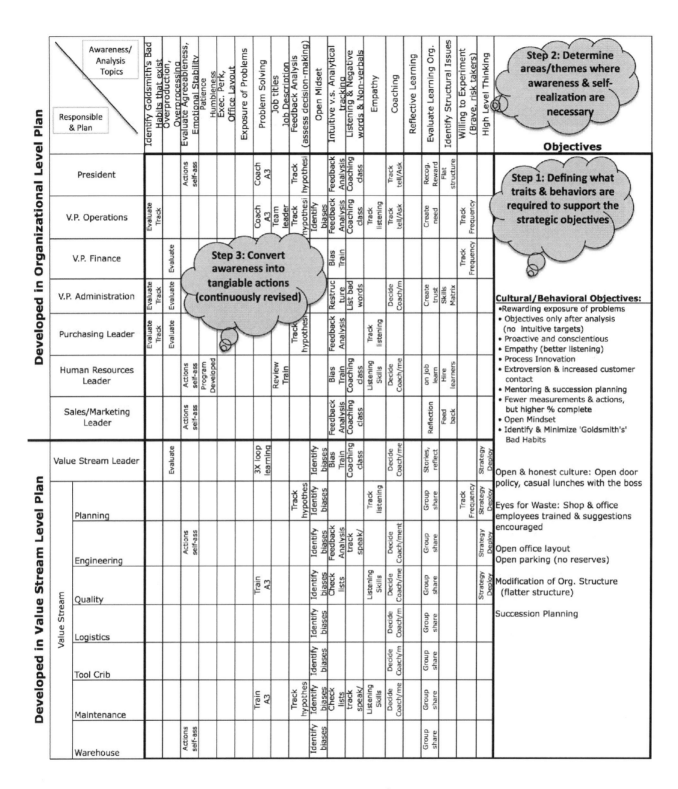

Figure 2.1: Cultural Transformation Plan

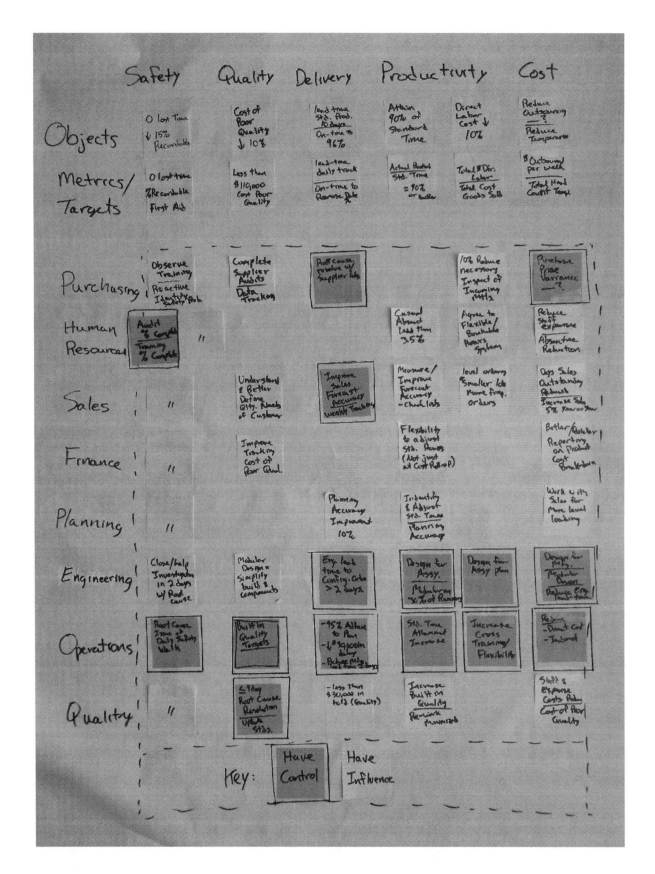

Figure 2.2: The Dynamics of a Team Working through Strategy Deployment

Do not be overwhelmed by the detail and complication, as the entire book is dedicated to the underlying organizational awareness that must take place in arriving at this seemingly complex visualization. The matrices by themselves hold little value, but the interaction in their development and follow-up are where I have witnessed some light bulbs blink to life—or at least glow a little brighter. Simplicity is key for understanding, communicating, and especially following-up, and although at first glance the matrixes may seem a bit busy, this is your yearly strategy and your Cultural Transformation Plan all in one visual that is fairly easy to follow. You can also review progress (PDCA) and realign as you go forward.

Consider *catch-ball* (a participative approach to decision-making, in which information and ideas go back and forth, allowing in-depth understanding and development, while gaining buy-in from all parties). Matrices like this can guide the catch-ball process because details are out in the open, which facilitates revisions and follow-up.

Catch-ball will be repeatedly referred to throughout this book, it is important to realize this is the main communication process employed in strategy deployment to agree upon actions (which are actually experiments) to achieve the goals. This catch-ball not only takes place vertically within the company but also horizontally, and how it gets started will differ depending on the current organizational structure. Catch-ball helps ensure everyone has a little '*skin in the game*'.

> *Note:* Early on in the process, someone external should professionally facilitate catch-ball as they will introduce neutrality.

Both deployed strategic objectives and their connection to a cultural transformation plan are required to make a change in mentality. Although every leader will be part of the development of the matrices and understand the interdependencies, the implementation is very manageable. Subsequent to further development, each leader should be focused only on his or her row, which that person developed and is responsible for (for example, look horizontally across the Sales row in Figure 2.1).

Even those companies whose success is based on the development of technology need to remember that higher levels of success come from a collaborative process that links market demands to the organization's plan. This is accomplished by involving your entire organization's human intellect in the design of that plan.

The remainder of this book is dedicated to the soft side of cultural change, as visualized in the matrices. The work begins with a clearly deployed strategy that is then combined with your Cultural Transformation Plan, and both are necessary in successfully implementing either improvement and/or breakthrough objectives. The self-criticalness required in identifying the necessary changes in your mentality or the errors caused by your judgments, for example, by your intuitive versus analytical thinking, are not easy. As such, you must understand the importance of this self-critical process throughout the discussions presented in this book.

Strategy Deployment: What It's Not

Strategy deployment is not a budget; instead, it is a form of your financial planning, although it can support the budget. Budgets are more reactive, reviewing performance and trying to account for variances. Strategy deployment is not throwing together 30 or more initiatives you think are important but will only dilute your limited resources. It is not telling people what to do. (I also don't like to hear it called policy deployment, because, for me, policy implies formality, government, bureaucracy, or a longtime frame that lacks flexibility.) It is not a form of cost cutting, as this does not stretch your capabilities, it usually destroys them. Strategy deployment is not creating a series of single events to tackle the many issues facing the organization. It has nothing to do with pushing non-negotiable targets onto the organization.

Strategy Deployment: What It Is

Strategy is more about synthesis among a team than it is about analytical planning. It involves developing buy-in through informal learning. Strategy deployment is a participative process to deploy your plan, focusing not only on the numbers but also on the processes being used to drive improvement, with strong follow-up (PDCA) that encourages learning and adjusting. Strategy provides an understanding and consensus of the organization's objectives and its future. It entails brutally removing many of the ideas (or pet projects) that you do not have either the resources, support, or the data (to confirm they will provide a sufficient rate of return) to pursue. Strategy will lead you to doing a few things effectively instead of many inconclusively, determining how to best use your scarce resources. It will drive process improvements, which will cut costs. It should also define those barriers preventing you from achieving the objectives and help you develop countermeasures.

An Overview of Strategy Deployment

Strategy deployment is a collaborative annual process (an annual process for the purpose of this book), which involves buy-in from all levels in establishing five or six key objectives. It is not appropriating resources, but driving resourcefulness through a sense of purpose, a shared dream. Strategy is not executable unless it is understood, and how better to understand then being part of the team that developed it? Although it is data driven, intuitive thoughts are brought into play. It details down to the level of action plans and relates the actions back up as to how they connect to the customer. A good strategy is reviewed, there is reflection, and there are revisions when necessary.

A successful strategy also contains plans of how it is to be deployed, and many of these detailed plans will be developed at a level outside the annual strategy deployment matrix you utilize as your guiding visual. An actual example of an annual strategy matrix taken from an organization in their first year of deployment is shown in Figure 2.3 (detailed departmental and individual action plans will be completed and maintained separately in each value stream). The catch-ball process shown here builds consensus and creates a more informal decision-making process, linking the strategies to the various levels within the organization. A primary function of catch-ball is for the preceding level to translate the objectives for the next level in a meaningful way in which they can relate; this translation will differ with the various levels. It also follows the principal that those closest to the work know it best and are in the best position to determine the plans to support the targets. (How to practically create buy-in when developing your strategy will be detailed in Chapter 3.)

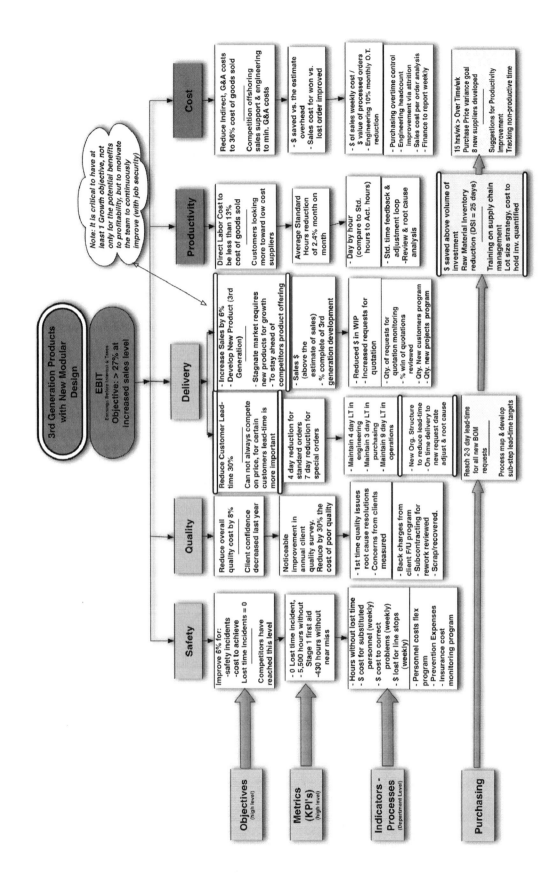

Figure 2.3: Strategy Deployment Matrix (top)

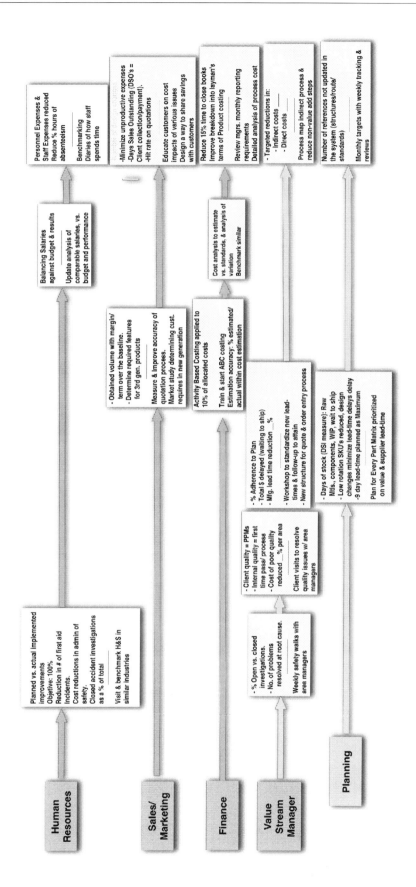

Figure 2.3: Strategy Deployment Matrix (middle)

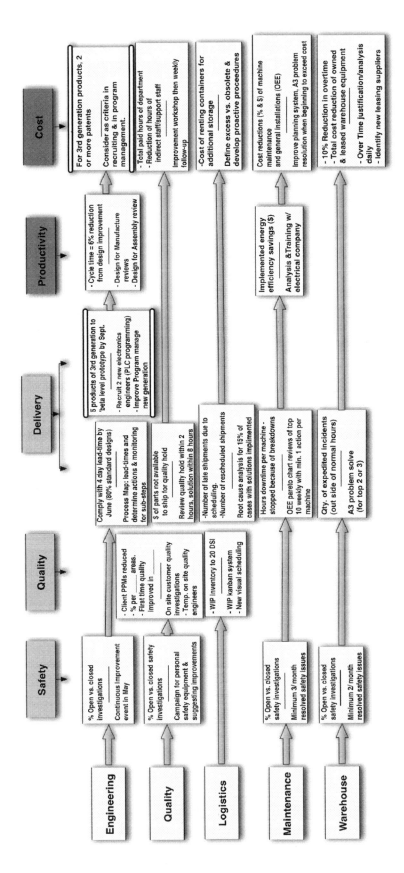

Figure 2.3: Strategy Deployment Matrix (bottom)

Naturally, a strategy that involves the big picture or long-term changes requires doing things differently; this equates to making a cultural transformation. In fact, this is the link between the matrices (refer to Figure 2.1), but you can't move the cart without the horse, which is why the strategy should come first. The similar formats for both matrices are recommended, as everyone must be part of identifying their changes in relation to the organization's objectives. To make these changes, you will also need to understand how you learn and how you become a learning organization, this is discussed after explaining the matrices.

Typical Reasons for Failure to Deploy a Strategy

Many organizations are not ready for the level of openness necessary to make a cultural change; they cannot come to terms with putting aside pet projects or managing more analytically instead of intuitively. They will struggle with the disciplined and frequent reviews, falling back to a command-and-control-style budget.

Organizations often claim they have been doing strategy deployment for years. If you are one of these, judge where you might be missing an enormous opportunity to drive change leadership after reading this chapter. I also encourage a quick reality check of how clearly your strategy is deployed and communicated by randomly asking five or ten of your teammates (from various levels and departments) what are the annual objectives in their departments and what improvement actions are they working on. When supporting organizations, I always ask this and frequently see a difference in top leadership's perception of how well the strategy is deployed. This leads me to believe that, in reality, many of these companies focus only on day-to-day survival. Some other common mistakes in traditional command-and-control strategy include:

- Objectives are vague and broad (usually determined intuitively)

- Objectives are *pushed* onto the organization as non-negotiable

- Only short-term measures are put into place, instead of initiatives with a customer focus and growth (i.e. no breakthrough objectives)

- Allowing a complacent culture instead of using this process in developing a culture that is not overly proud, causing them to neglect opportunities

- Creating a series of individual events ("one-offs") for specific areas

- Too many objectives (includes everyone's wish lists and pet projects)

- It becomes only a plan to deploy lean tools or projects for quick, high-impact results that are not sustainable

For those who can do it, these cross-functional conversations and alignments not only engage all departments in understanding their objectives, but also minimize the *silo effect* (only focusing on optimizing your department, often at the expense of the whole organization), by understanding the relational impact between the various processes and actions being planned. This flexible system that instills discipline to follow-up and learn.

Why Use the Strategy Deployment Matrix?

There are many formats in which strategy deployment manifests itself, and I have tried quite a few, although I find building this strategy deployment matrix (refer to Figure 2.2 or 2.3) is an easy way to create the dynamics and flexibility necessary to involve all the levels in a two-way process that secures buy in. The strategy deployment matrix should be constructed using Post-it Notes on a large roll of paper; this allows it to develop in steps, along with encouraging flexibility and comfort while brainstorming and revising. It demonstrates where interdepartmental relationships exist and how the objectives complement one another; the blank quadrants also show where no linkage was determined. The strategy deployment matrix is formed with rows and columns, creating considerable flexibility, but I will take you through what typically works best in deploying this basic format. Beginning with a brief introduction, start at the top level, shown by the first 3 rows in Figure 2.3. Each cell/box at the top should be split, containing an objective as well as the reason or necessity for that objective—this drives the communication and insight through the various levels. This dialogue should connect the importance of the objectives in terms of customers and markets; this is critical, as it will improve the lower-level understanding and strategies while reducing the struggle, although you should also be flexible: if the lower-level cannot support the upper-level strategies, your catch-ball process must allow for realignment. A *strategic decision* can be defined as having significant consequences and placing demands on resources; therefore, it is critical that it is discussed and visualized in front of everyone and includes the entire team's buy in.

Another method to guide and visualize strategy deployment is the Strategy Deployment X-matrix supported by various levels of A3 Problem Solving (11×17 piece of paper). I encourage A3 thinking and believe that it should be combined with the strategy deployment matrix being presented. It is the best way for the teams to work through developing the processes and actions that will support the matrix in this book. I have included a simple example of A3 thinking (applied to strategy deployment) in Appendix B. There are various books like Thomas Jackson's, *Hoshin Kanri for the Lean Enterprise*[4] , which can guide you through the use of these A3 formats .

When the X-matrix (see Figure 2.4) is utilized in strategy deployment, its primary benefit is to demonstrate the relationship between objectives, key projects, targeted goals/metrics, and annual objectives. The advantage of this format is you can see where a relationship exists between the high-level objectives and the details of the selected projects. When utilizing the X-matrix to deploy strategy you typically employ a number of these matrices at various levels and functional responsibilities throughout the organization. These are supported by various formats of A3, for example you can have one for intelligence gathering, another for the team to plan an action or strategy, or one for a status report, these can be referred to as A3-I, A3-T and A3-SR respectively.

I often find that leaders and team members have some trouble relating to the X-matrix, and that it is not as flexible in its development. It does not always clearly specify why the high-level objectives are necessary or help clearly relate how the various processes will be measured and will add to the overall targeted results (metrics). In the X-matrix where you see the triangle, square or X, choosing the appropriate symbols becomes more of a tick-the-box exercise. There is no definitive structure to facilitate a deeper discussion with each department of whether they can have *control* or *influence* concerning the various objectives, or what measurements/indicators could be utilized and what actions should be taken, as is performed when using the recommended post-it matrix (figure 2.2).

I find the best results are achieved by first using the strategy deployment matrix (from this book) annually to flush out all possible relationships of control and influence in support the objectives and then try putting this information into the X-matrix to see if it identifies additional relationships. I have included the following example of an X-matrix so you can consider the rewards of utilizing it in conjunction with the strategy deployment matrix present in Chapters 2 and 3.

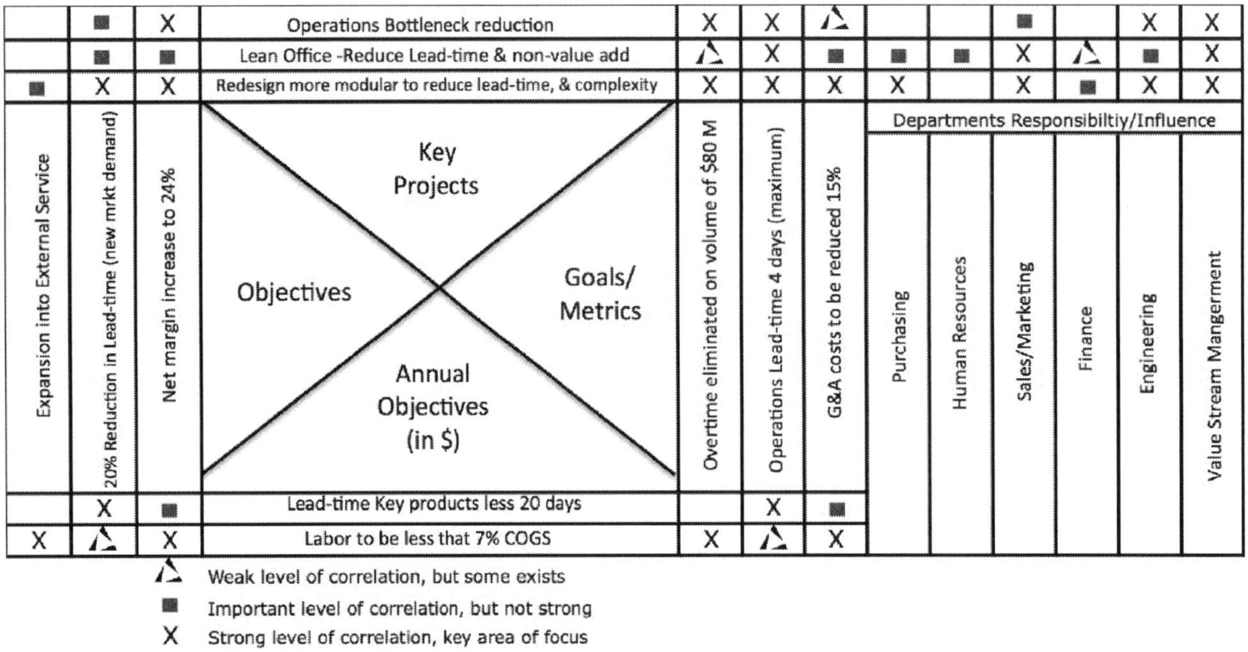

A	B	C	Key Projects / Objectives / Goals-Metrics / Annual Objectives (in $)	D	E	F	Purchasing	Human Resources	Sales/Marketing	Finance	Engineering	Value Stream Mangerment
	■	X	Operations Bottleneck reduction	X	X	▲			■		X	X
	■	■	Lean Office -Reduce Lead-time & non-value add	▲	X	■	■	■	X	▲	■	X
■	X	X	Redesign more modular to reduce lead-time, & complexity	X	X	X	X		X	■	X	X
			Key Projects / *Objectives* / *Goals/Metrics* / *Annual Objectives (in $)*						Departments Responsibiltiy/Influence			
	X	■	Lead-time Key products less 20 days		X	■						
X	▲	X	Labor to be less that 7% COGS	X	▲	X						

Column headers (left to right): Expansion into External Service · 20% Reduction in Lead-time (new mrkt demand) · Net margin increase to 24% · [center X: Key Projects, Objectives, Goals/Metrics, Annual Objectives (in $)] · Overtime eliminated on volume of $80 M · Operations Lead-time 4 days (maximum) · G&A costs to be reduced 15% · Purchasing · Human Resources · Sales/Marketing · Finance · Engineering · Value Stream Mangerment

▲ Weak level of correlation, but some exists
■ Important level of correlation, but not strong
X Strong level of correlation, key area of focus

Figure 2.4 Strategy Deployment X-Matrix

The clear advantages I have witnessed when teams construct the strategy deployment matrix displayed in Figures 2.2 and 2.3 are:

- Its flexibility (Post-its Notes on brown paper) encourages cross-functional discussions, brainstorming, and give and take.

- It encourages communication and guides you through developing and communicating the need for change, as well as facilitates revising and updating (this is done in the Objectives row).

- Completing the columns and rows clarifies the interrelationships and makes the links clear (wherever a Post-its get placed), versus where no link exists (no Post-its are located). It provides a structure to question each cell (Post-it) for whether a relationship exists.

- Empty fields indicate there was neither *control* nor *influence* between that objective and the particular department (although the strategy deployment matrix guides in inquiring whether there is a relationship at every cell).

- It realizes the necessity of both incremental improvements and breakthrough objectives and distinguishes between them (the double lines indicate breakthrough objectives in Figure 2.3).

- It facilitates the process of playing catch-ball through the various levels (top-down), moving first through rows and then down the columns.

- The split boxes in the top of the strategy deployment matrix, do the following:

  o In the objectives row: Clarifies the top level objectives and what necessitates the target (i.e. customer or market requirements).

  o In the indicators-processes row: Department level indicators support high level metrics and are encouraged to quantify how the indicator will be measured or improved.

- The split boxes in the body of the strategy deployment matrix, do the following:

  o In the departmental rows: The top of each box contains the measurements or indicators the department will try utilizing to support the top-level metric, and the bottom of each box guides you to consider the actions that support improving that indicator (which is often overlooked when developing strategies).

- The strategy deployment matrix clarifies "how will the change affect me?" by showing what objectives, processes, and actions are related to each department, and this is then developed in more detail on the team level boards (not shown).

- A disciplined PDCA cycle is easier to maintain with the strategy deployment matrix. Also learnings and changes are encouraged and simplified (this can be visually noted on the strategy deployment matrix—see Chapter 3).

- By limiting the number of columns, you keep the focus on a small number of customer-related objectives that can be supported by your available resources.

All these advantages are discussed in detail in Chapter 3.

Realistic versus Ideal Implementation

You can read certain books on strategy deployment and walk away thinking the concepts are straightforward, but I imagine you also know your organization and its reluctance to change. Therefore, instead of being an idealist, let's talk about what works when trying to introduce strategy deployment. First you must consider this a long term commitment. Before you have a robust process in place normally requires three cycles (three years) prior to finding how the process will yield the best results in your company. Every organization will adjust and continuously improve the method, and this should be encouraged. Moving away from a results-driven organization to focusing on processes (knowing they drive results) is unlikely to happen quickly, no matter how insightful you become reading books or talking to experts. It is far better to introduce a process while linking it to the results (as done in the split boxes in the body of the strategy deployment matrix), since your organizational culture can likely relate to this.

If you are utilizing an annual budget, I do not recommend a dramatic switch in the beginning from budgeting to only utilizing strategy deployment. I find drastic change is difficult to support; therefore, continue with your budget while introducing strategy deployment and ensure that you reflect and learn the differences. Document the cultural challenges you encounter, as you can likely identify improvement steps after reading this book and incorporate them into your Cultural Transformation Plan. Considering the cart-before-the-horse analogy, I am strongly suggesting strategy deployment first, followed promptly by a Cultural Transformation Plan. (Experience has shown that undesirable personal traits displayed/identified during the strategy deployment process are helpful when considering that areas which require improvement in the Cultural Transformation Plan.)

Additional Reasons Strategy Deployment Fails

Before going into detail in Chapter 3 about the dynamics of constructing the strategy deployment matrix, consider some additional reasons why strategy deployment falls short:

- The organization is overwhelmed with the day-to-day, with a lack of time for breakthrough objectives.

- If your organizational culture sees asking "why?" as disruptive, then the objectives will be pushed downward without explanation and the expectation is they will be accepted on faith, this leads to creating non-negotiable objectives. Another way to say this: the organization believes a brilliant strategy should not be questioned or changed

- You will see the silo effect of improving metrics in isolation, without understanding or having responsibility for the linkage to other departments, customers, or other measurements, especially given that some measurements have to work in opposition, (i.e. reducing inventory while simultaneously improving on-time delivery).

- There is a lack of data analysis when creating top level or departmental objectives (intuitive instead of analytical; unrealistic stretch targets arbitrarily created without involvement or buy-in).

- There either are not enough reviews or there is not any learning from root cause analysis.

- No catch-ball or team established objectives, so those objectives tend not to be customer focused or drive sustained profitability.

- Members are allowed to throw in their wish lists instead of brutally focusing on a few areas to effectively improve.

- Your objectives do not focus on relieving team member's struggles.

The strategy deployment matrix we are about to talk through is not a *requirement* of strategy deployment, but I have not come across a simpler way to visualize, develop, communicate, and follow-up on strategic objectives. You are trying to create a method of informal learning versus more rigid planning based only on analysis. The Japanese phrase for strategy deployment is *Hoshin Kanri,* which I define as traditional strategy deployment, but with a heavy emphasis on PDCA (plan, do, check, act). When most explain Hoshin, they speak about aligning the organization with *True North*, which is a good metaphor to keep in mind for your strategy deployment, as many get lost in the day-to-day firefighting. This is another reason I find the strategy deployment matrix an ideal format, as it makes frequent follow-up and changes easy (not that you want to continuously change, but there is a reality to learning and adjusting the plan). Remember that the minute team members perceive a lack of interest in the strategy, everything returns to just achieving day-to-day results. In command-and-control environments, management typically only takes notice or control when the desired results are not achieved; strategy deployment instead focuses on the process of improvement.

Summary

To make a successful and sustainable culture, you must begin with properly deploying your annual strategy. This begins your cultural change, as this is not a strategy that is pushed from top-down (in the case of creating non-negotiable objectives, believing this will focus the organization on execution instead of questioning the goals); instead, it is a clarification of *why* high-level objectives are important to the customer, followed by two way discussions at each level as to how they can support these top-level goals and what actions are necessary. Once strategic objectives are clear and supported at each level in the organization, you can identify what soft issues need to be changed in the mentalities of the leadership team, in order to reach the objectives. This awareness and identification of the traits and behaviors requiring change, becomes your Cultural Transformation Plan (outlined in Chapter 5).

CHAPTER 3

Implementing the Strategy Deployment Matrix

Because implementing strategy deployment holistically is not the focus of this book, I am likely misleading you if one is to assume the strategy deployment matrix utilized and developed in this chapter is the concept in its entirety. Although it is a critical portion of the strategic work (an *annual* strategy deployment for a single location), it does not consider the long term vision (a three- to five-year plan). Therefore if you are part of a large organization with multiple locations or do not have clear long term strategic vision, I encourage you and members of your team to acquire this additional awareness and knowledge through additional reading, conferences, or seminars.

Roles and Responsibilities

When working through strategy development, there are different roles and responsibilities for the various levels. I feel it is the top leadership's responsibility to understand how the global market is changing and what new competitors and factors are entering the market-place, and then create five or six key objectives. In addition, top leadership should communicate how complacency in today's dynamic world will lead to failure. All the while, top leadership must also ensure that the team understands they now have two responsibilities simultaneously: performing the day-to-day tasks while moving toward the future. I bring this responsibility of communication to the forefront, as it is one area of the strategy deployment matrix (see the first three rows in Figure 3.1) that should be completed up front and usually involves the leadership team, once appreciably aligned they can deploy to the next level. When the high level objectives and measurements are settled, you are ready to enter discussions with your departmental leadership teams, during which they must determine whether they can identify methods and actions to either support the top level objectives or consideration must be given to revising them.

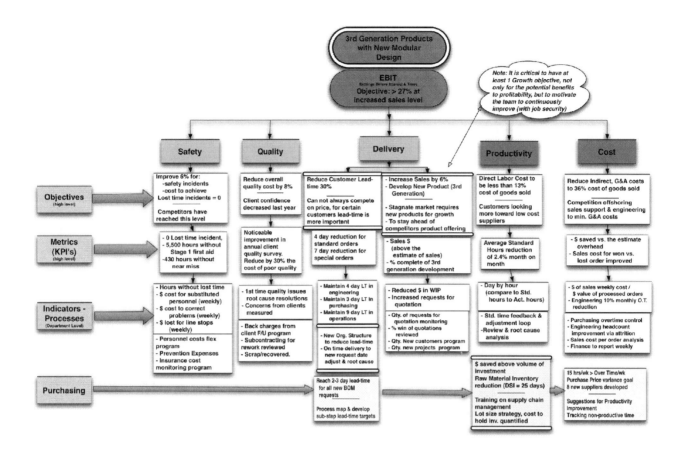

Figure 3.1: Top Three Rows of Strategy Deployment Matrix

The remainder of this chapter is the how-to guide for building the strategy deployment matrix. During this process, many of your leaders' traits and behaviors, including bad habits, are likely to be displayed; therefore, it is worthwhile to read this entire book before beginning any additional work on your strategy deployment, as you will be in a better position to consider additional actions to overcome these bad habits. Having a Cultural Transformation Plan first (see Chapter 5) would improve these types of problems in the process, but as mentioned in Chapter 2, you want to complete your strategy deployment first. However, you may read this entire book and decide for your organization to be successful, that you need to first develop your Cultural Transformation Plan and begin working through it before your team's traits and behaviors will be prepared to give strategy deployment the open focus it deserves. Although I've experienced that approach, I do believe that strategy deployment followed by a Cultural Transformation Plan is the best practice.

Strategy Deployment Matrix: a How-to Guide

The how-to discussion in this section is based on SMEs (small and medium enterprises) utilizing a strategy-deployment matrix to structure, communicate, and deploy only their annual strategy. This is an important distinction to make because complete strategy deployment (or Hoshin Kanri) for a *Fortune* 500 company will have additional considerations. Again I refer you to more complete guides of the entire strategy deployment processes, like the one previously recommended in Chapter 2.

More successful change happens when it starts with small improvements, instead of being driven as a corporate wide objective. For this reason, creating a plant-level strategy matrix is the ideal scope. You just need to remember that, to begin with, it is mostly about hypotheses and learning, and this is best done by first focusing on small and continuous improvements instead of on a quick hit home run.

As you move from top to bottom of the strategy deployment matrix, we want to think and focus in two areas:

- **Improvement objectives:** target continuous improvement (based on analysis) for a few critical areas. *Note:* This is critical until your business fundamentals are in place.

- **Breakthrough objectives:** thinking out of the box; not only trying to make a fit between your current resources, skills, technologies, and budgets to what you perceive are the upcoming opportunities, but also to stretch and reach breakthroughs. *Note:* This comes after proving we can deploy and sustain improvement objectives.

We assume this strategy deployment matrix is being developed for the single site level, not for a multi-plant or multi-division organization. Also I would rather *not* start with defining the mission or values, typically a critical element of strategy deployment. And, in the same way, translating the vision into a long-range (multi-year) plan will *not* be incorporated. Let's start, instead, at the annual planning level for our single site. This is a data-driven process, although the detailed techniques for defining the current situation (i.e. sales trends, competitors trends, industry trends, new technology, customer satisfaction and expectations, core organizational competencies, and so on) will not be explained, as there are many excellent publications that cover these.

Note: Although neither corporate or team mission statements are being covered in this book, one example of a team statement that has evolved with a few organizations I have supported and really reinforces Toyota's culture is something like, "My responsibilities include continuously improving our processes," as this reinforces a culture where everyone is responsible for improvements, anywhere they can have an effect, in addition to their day-to-day responsibilities. It connects to a customer focus, and it is specific, achievable, and motivating, like a good mission statement should be. I include this only because most mission and vision statements I see plastered in the lobbies appear to be meaningful only to those who proudly created them, although they sound irrelevant to most team members.

Therefore, your starting point is having the current situation defined (both within your external and internal environments), and we will assume it is supported by analysis (marketing data) and that upper management accepts this information as substantiated and accurate. We will also assume your mission is clear and that the long-range plan is agreed upon. Your top management will start this annual planning process a few months before the next financial year begins. Naturally it is easier to align the time span for the strategic plan with your financial year, which has been the purpose and process behind the budget for many organizations. So if you utilize a budgeting process, this is where you make the link.

Remember my recommendation is that if you are currently utilizing a budget, it will be easier culturally to begin strategy deployment while simultaneously maintaining the budget. Ideally, there will be more focus, effort and follow-up with the strategy deployment than that which continues in the budgeting process. The budget is more of a day-to-day operating system (maintaining the status quo), where strategy deployment is defining the processes that will lead to breakthrough objectives. The idealists might suggest forgetting the budget and putting all your effort into the strategy, but the realists know that organizational cultural and habits are deeply ingrained and require a gradual transition that incorporates awareness and learning.

I suggest taking the opportunity, during the first years of utilizing strategy deployment, to use both a financial budget and deployment of your strategy, and to see it as a period of reflection and learning. I recommend making this a structured reflection connected with your follow-ups of the strategy deployment.

Begin your strategy deployment by reflecting on last year's strategy (assuming you had one and it was documented) and review what went right and what went wrong. In Chapter 5, I discuss how to incorporate *feedback analysis,* an old and established technique, but suffice it to say, all scientific methods involve a hypothesis (ideally written down) and later a comparison to what actually happened, followed by reflective learning to improve your methods. Using feedback analysis to learn is better then just starting the new strategy with the hope that this year will turn out better than the last.

Drafting the Top Portion of the Strategy Deployment Matrix

Although strategy deployment is not necessarily a top-down approach, the only way to start your annual strategy is by defining top-level priorities. Later, your catch-ball process will question whether you can fulfill these objectives—and confirm that they can be met. Traditionally top-level objectives are for either a growth purpose or simply to ensure survival. In a turbulent environment, some may intuitively create stretch goals that push the team outside their comfort zone, although intuitive goals (created without a feasibility analysis) or stretch targets that are unrealistic can be very demotivating (you want aggressive and hard to reach goals, but you don't want targets developed without engagement and pushed onto someone). When a team is given a predetermined objective based on instinct, not on analysis, the team's acceptance differs depending whether the boss is in- or outside of the room. If he or she is present, there is a lot of head nodding in support of the objective; if the leader is not present, it quickly becomes apparent when the team was not part of developing the goal, and they both question its attainability and lack confidence in its feasibility.

Recently, while I was working with the senior leadership of an Australian defense contractor, it became apparent that the boss's goals were not being supported. This lack of buy-in manifested itself as we began to quantify what an established cost target meant in terms of the necessary actions (i.e. we went to where the value was being added; going to *gemba*), and worked through the details necessary to reach the target. When comparing what the team agreed was possible (based on data gathering and the analysis we performed) with what the boss had set as the target, eyes rolled in an "I told you so" fashion, indicating the boss's intuitive targets had no basis in reality and were not supported by the team. Obviously, this was a top down approach, where the boss set targets on his own. His team was expected to rally around these non-negotiable objectives and use all available means to achieve them. The final conclusion, after analytically problem solving, brainstorming, and thinking outside the box, was to suggest a different target that had supporting processes and actions, which the team felt they could attain with significant effort (still it required pushing their limits).

Knowing now what you don't want to do, let's discuss the first step of what you need to do in a culture change. You want a *top leadership team* to take the data defining the current situation (sales trends, competitors trends, industry trends, new technology, customer satisfaction and expectations, core organizational competencies, and so on) and define the top-level bubbles in the strategy deployment matrix (shown by the two ovals in Figure 3.1). If top leadership is out of touch with the customer, the marketing information introduced in the current-state analysis should help. In this actual example (from the organization's first year of strategy deployment) there are two objectives: a *breakthrough* (displayed with the double lined bold ring) of creating a new modular design, and an *improvement objective* of obtaining greater than 27% earnings before interest and tax (EBIT). Most of strategy deployment enthusiasts love to throw around only planning for breakthrough objectives, citing these as necessary for survival in the modern business world. The reality is you do need these to be very successful, but most companies can focus only on one or two breakthroughs while the remaining objectives should focus on the incremental day-to-day improvements. So I recommend a mix, and to help in visualizing this mix, I have found it helpful to distinguish them on the strategy deployment matrix (in this case, with the double line encircling them).

Generally, it is not practical or logical to involve your entire team in setting high-level objectives (unless you are part of a very small or flat organization), although the other leaders should be involved in verifying whether these are obtainable objectives and which processes and actions are necessary in reaching them. Therefore, drafting or proposing high-level goals, and clarifying why they are necessary or reasonable expectations, is the first responsibility of top leadership in this process. They should be firm but flexible with these; therefore, they should be developed with Post-it notes and presented to the next level through a two-way catch-ball process. Remember that Post-its, by their nature, create a flexible discussion and demonstrate that the results are not cast in stone for the next leadership level. Although 3M invented Post-its by accident, it appears they were destined to become an important working tool in a continuous improvement journey!

If top management is out of touch with the front-line issues and proposes dream-level objectives, the strategy deployment matrix will bring them back to reality as the department and team levels struggle to develop action plans in support of the goals.

If you are part of a multiple-site business, or a division within a larger entity, the two ovals at the top of Figure 3.1 would be the key goals that are proposed from the level above the site manager; in other words, this is what would be necessary from this location in order to support the corporate objectives. There would be some catch-ball between corporate leadership and the top site-level leadership to reach agreement, and then the deployment via catch-ball would start working its way through the site's organization. A key function of catch-ball as you deploy through the various layers is for the previous level to translate the objectives for the next level, so they are insightful and have meaning. (This entire process is covered in detail in other books discussing strategy deployment in larger corporations.)

These top level bubbles are not only the link to the vision (there is the three- to five-year plan that is necessary but not included in the strategy deployment matrix); they are also there as a focus and communication tool. As the catch-ball moves down through the levels, each layer must communicate and then re-communicate the vision to the team members and discuss why it is important in terms of growth.

Periodically included within either the top ovals or the objectives row are high-level strategies that apply to only a few parts of the organization. For example, imagine you are targeting growth through acquisitions; the plan might be that these new divisions will continue to be operated as separate entities and will only have some periodic management and financial reporting back to the existing organization. This is unlikely to have an impact on departments like operations or value-stream managers, but you should include these plans in the strategy deployment matrix, as it will help in questioning all links (control and influence) and the impacts. For example, you might be planning not to incorporate the newly acquired division's sales team with the existing sales group, but by questioning whether any relationship exists, leaders may discover some pull-through sales opportunities, ensuring others are motivated to create the demand for sales of your product because they themselves will somehow profit, creating a win-win situation.

The Objectives Row

Now let's move from the two top-level ovals to the five or six objectives in the first row that create the strategic intent. (The Objectives row with its six columns is shown in Figure 3.1.) This row is not only meant to include breakthroughs but also improvement objectives (those that are more in line with annual continuous improvement). These objectives will be broken into more detail in the next two rows, the Metrics and the Indicator-Process rows. You can debate the necessity of all three rows, but I find more often than not that teams are comfortable and feel clearer in communicating within the organization when all three rows are utilized.

Using safety, productivity, quality, delivery, and cost as the categories for creating the columns is only one option, although doing so keeps the high-level objectives to a manageable size and typically accounts for what is critical in an organization. This is not all-inclusive, and you need to also consider a balanced score card, which includes the four basic types of measurement: financial measures, customer measures, internal business (process) measures, and innovation and learning measures. The last category is often overlooked, but it is key in developing breakthroughs. All this is to say that you don't want to utilize this example as a rigid format; instead, it needs to encompass what is important to your organization.

Note: All suggestions and formats in this book should be used as a guideline, in other words: *Don't adopt it, instead adapt it.*

Starting at the top, think in two directions: 1) how are you going to measure success, and 2) either what key process are you going to use to get there or why is this necessary. Most boxes in the strategy deployment matrix are split into these two categories, and I strongly recommend this to drive the thinking of the *what* and, more importantly, the *how or why*. Here, however, is where my experience deviates slightly from the strategy deployment purists. They emphasize more the processes and actions used in your strategy, and put less focus on targets. Anyone will agree that processes and actions are critical, yet traditional strategic planning and budgets focus mostly on the targets. I concur that the process to get there is most important, but the measurement is what makes the business viable for the future. Therefore, the beauty of the strategy deployment matrix is you can use it to guide the creation of both measures and the processes (or actions) at each step.

Putting the safety column first is important and demonstrates the right priority to the team, followed by quality (warranty, customer calls) and delivery (percent lost sales, percent cancellations for being late), as those are external, customer measurements that are felt each day. Finally, productivity and cost are put as internal measures and, although many will say "nowadays it's only price, price, and price," costs tend to improve dramatically when you get quality products and delivery correct. Productivity and cost (material/

labor costs, supplies and mark-up) are fundamentally internal metrics that don't always translate directly into the price paid by the customer, as an external measure for cost you can look at lost sales due to price. If your quality or delivery are miserable, you never get to have the discussion about price; therefore, they precede the internal measures. In the Objectives row, propose the top-level goals for these categories—some may be quantifiable, while others may not. The second half the box should be the reason for either this breakthrough or improvement objective; this is how you will communicate its importance to the organization. Glancing through Figure 3.1 (which is a real-company's work in progress), the Objectives row is a mix of two breakthroughs, while the remaining are classified as improvement objectives (distinguished by the single or double lines). It can be a gray area as to what is a breakthrough and what is an improvement goal, and I have no definitive answer: every team I work with comes to its own understanding. I feel the concept is important, however, because you do not just want to survive, you also want to work on quantum leaps. In this example, it was not going to be business as usual in attaining a 30 percent reduction in customer lead-time, but that reduction was critical to be able to move away from purely competing on price. This was also considered a breakthrough because of the realization that this would require a new structure. If you identify more than a few break through objectives there are prioritization matrices available to guide you in selecting the most appropriate and manageable ones.

Lead-time is a great example of an objective that is not directly a cost cutting goal but has a strong correlation. The economics of relating an improvement in lead-time to cost and profit can be a challenge, but one large corporation estimated that by cutting its lead-time in half it would result in a 10-15% reduction in operating costs for capital equipment and manufacturing. Not to mention the potential sales increase, as this might allow you to serve new markets and customers.

The other breakthrough was moving on to a third-generation design, as this was going to require new resources (with a different skill set) to be brought into the engineering department. So you can conclude that the criterion that distinguishes a breakthrough is when either:

- a new structure is required or

- new resources are required

You Must Have at Least One Growth Objective

A critical type of objective that is required for any organization focused on continuous improvement is some form of a *growth target*. If you want to encourage people to improve, they need the security of knowing how productivity gains will be utilized, instead of fearing they might find themselves out of a job. So instead of making only hollow statements about no one losing their jobs due to improvements, encourage continuous improvement by deploying growth targets in the strategy deployment matrix (clarifying how time saving improvements can be profitably utilized). These could be straightforward goals like reducing the amount of outsourcing or reducing the number of temporary employees. And they don't need necessarily need to be about expansion and could instead identify an overall savings to the organization as resources become available. These should not only be continuously reinforced during the catch-ball process in the strategy deployment, but also at all times to encourage people to openly identify waste and propose solutions.

The "Why" is Vital to the Organization

The lower portion of the Post-its (boxes) in this row are an opportunity for leadership to convince the organization of the objective's importance in the customer's eyes. Remember that many inside the organization's walls do not have direct contact with the market or customers and are not privy to the data gathered in establishing the current situation, or the reasons change is required. I recommend the strategy deployment matrix remain a living document visualized throughout the organization, as it is meant to be a transparent method to ensure goals are continually communicated and clarified.

The Metrics Row

The Metrics row is where you want to question your existing metrics (KPIs) and understand whether those will lead to breakthroughs or are sufficient in just maintaining what we have always done. I want to provide a few examples here, as it is often critical in cultural transformations to revamp your measurements, and the strategy deployment matrix is the perfect structure to ensure you systematically question whether existing metrics should be replaced with improved KPIs, and then linking those KPIs to improvement ideas.

Since you don't want to use a measure that doesn't accomplish its intended purpose, you want to be clear on your intended goal and not use an existing metric out of emotion or historical significance. This makes it likely that you will revise your metrics as a result of this process. Metrics must also be compared to some meaningful standard; otherwise they hold no consequence. Remember that some key metrics work in opposite directions, and your objective is to balance and optimize based on your situation—for example, improving lead-time (or on-time-delivery) while maintaining or reducing your inventory level. These are not easy goals to achieve in tandem, but you increase your chances of success if you use the correct metrics and truly understand the relationship between the measurement and the influences. (This is explained in more detail in the following example on the correct measurement for inventory.)

Good metrics always help in problem solving or at least in highlighting the causes of the issues you face. As an example, take two key areas affecting cash flow that were brought to the forefront of every business's attention during the global financial crisis, when banks tightened up credit: inventory and receivables.

Inventory

Let's first look at inventory and discuss traditional units of measure: some use dollars while others use units (pieces, tons, and the like). As an example, imagine an organization currently has $10 million of raw material inventory.

If you read "$10 million of raw material inventory" and intuitively believe this is terrible, you may need to think a little more analytically. (If instead you were thinking, "it depends," you're on the right track!) If the business I am referring to has $1 billion in sales turnover each year, that $10 million of inventory would likely put them into a world-class category on inventory management. On the other hand, if the business has sales of $10 million annually, this would equate to having one year or more of raw material inventory, signifying there is a lot of opportunity for improvement. So we see that dollars of inventory is a poor measurement, if taken in isolation. Another more progressive and improved unit of measure is inventory turns (annual turn rate of inventory), but the downside is that this number can be measured only in relative terms. For example, if I currently have a turn rate of 5.7, that must be compared to a prior period to have any significance. Inventory turns aren't bad, but we must think a little deeper to find a measure that can be directly compared to a standard.

Let's think one step further: why have any inventory at all? That's right, why not just get rid of it all together? Well, there are quite a few reasons for inventory but the two most important are 1) to cover for lead-time and 2) because of the minimum lot size (or economic order quantity).

Now what unit is lead-time in? Normally it is measured in days, and although minimum lot sizes will usually be in pieces or tons, knowing your normal usage, you can convert this to days. Therefore, if the two most critical reasons to have any inventory can be measured in days, what should we measure inventory in? Hopefully you are thinking "days." There is a measure referred to as DSI (days sales inventory) and it is calculated this way:

DSI = average inventory / cost of sales per day

(This is the inverse ratio of inventory turn rate.) Now you have an inventory measurement in the unit of days, and everyone understands what a day is and can compare it to the days of supplier lead-time or days of manufacturing lead-time and start to understand the magnitude and cause of the problem. Better yet is you now can compare to a standard (i.e. days of lead-time) and know where to focus your efforts (remember that a good metric should be easy to align with a logical standard and should point you in the direction of what action to take). You can calculate a DSI for each product where you have a high inventory value and compare this to its lead-time, and begin improving where you have large differences (i.e. a plan for every part)

Receivables

The same discussion applies to measuring your accounts receivable: some measure in how many dollars are hanging out there, while others measure A/R aging, bad debt expenses, and so on. As an alternative, some utilize DSO (days sales outstanding). This takes you to speaking in days, which means you can compare this to a standard: the days in your terms and conditions from your various clients.

Although this metric has other critical aspects, the DSO measurement should start the clock ticking immediately when the product ships or the service is realized, not from when the invoice is issued. You might have a significant delay (caused by a number of processes or departments) between providing the service and the accounts department creating the invoice, and that opportunity for improvement should not be overlooked, as it is very much in your control, and often is disregarded if the correct metric is not understood and correctly applied.

Overall Equipment Effectiveness

As this is such a critical point, I want to provide one more example from the production environment. The following measurement is excellent for numerous reasons, but one of its strengths not often discussed is the linking of a non-financial measurement to the financials, and this is a key part of strategy deployment. Most high level measurements in an organization start in financial terms, but as you work through departmental and team levels, you should look for nonfinancial metrics and indicators that you can effect and understand the influence on your overall viability and profitability.

Overall equipment effectiveness (OEE) is like a standardized and inclusive way to understand your downtime on a process, though it should be applied only where an automatically regulated cycle time exists (i.e. an automatic cycling machine is contained somewhere in the flow). It is calculated considering the multiplying effect: OEE = availability x performance x quality. Although one or more of the components may be performing well, you get paid only based on how often a good part comes out of the process; in other words, your OEE is the percent of time you make money, and when any of the three multipliers is suboptimal, your profitability is effected. Further, the performance (in the equation), which is basically the difference between the planned and the actual speed at which the process is operating, should be based on the standard speed you determined for your process when you set the price (and margin); therefore, you are now directly connected to the financial measurement. For any process, you can also calculate what a 1 percent OEE improvement is worth in profitability, weekly or monthly. If you have processes that incorporate an automatically controlled cycle time and are not using this metric, you might want to learn more: www.oee.com is a good place to start.

I hope these examples clarify the old adage, "what you measure is what you get" or "if it doesn't get measured, it doesn't get improved." In the strategy deployment matrix, the Departmental rows will not always contain quantifiable goals and, even when they do, these should be proposals that are confirmed through catch-ball, analyzed, and linked to action plans. They should not be goals the boss intuitively dreams up, but ones that push the team beyond their comfort zone, they are confirmed and revised based on lots of hard work and discussions, analysis, and are associated with a measurement. But you have to determine a starting point, and if you can link an objective to what is required for success or what has been accomplished in the market, this can be a good beginning. Remember the new paradigm in this methodology is the clarification of *why* this is important and the buy-in of how it can be accomplished, instead of pushing non-negotiable objectives onto the organization. So don't tread lightly or quickly through metrics and do not assume the measurements that brought you to this point are the best going forward in your dynamic environment.

The Indicators/Processes Row

Another important row, the Indicators-Processes row, often requires a form of gemba (go to the real place where the value is added) to develop a realistic proposal. You can think in two parts (represented by either two Post-its or a split box in this row—see Figure 3.1):

- The first part of the cell should contain the indicators, the *leading indicators* that will lead to improving this metric or objective.

- The second part of the cell is to capture the projects or programs the team feels need to change or be developed at an organizational level to accomplish the objectives in this column.

To understand indicators, you first need to comprehend the difference between metrics and indicators and ideally be working with leading indicators.

- A *metric* quantifies a result against a standard at a point in time. Therefore, a metric is somewhat historic, financial metrics being some of the worst, as they are principally historic and often verified only monthly.

- An *indicator*—and you should speak in terms of *leading indicators*—can be used to predict a trend (usually short term) and usually changes well before the metric it is linked to.

Ideally, each metric (more of a historical figure) is linked to one or more leading indicators (real-time gauges), indicating which direction the metric will move. Therefore, you want a combination of metrics and indicators. I find it best if you have a few key metrics (as human focus becomes diluted and chaotic if a person is to focus on more that four or five metrics simultaneously), and you can add and subtract leading indicators, as they either help or hurt your efforts. Another term I like but can add to the confusion is KPI (key performance indicator), as by its definition it is a performance measure (which I associate with a metric), but uses the word indicator in the acronym. So, it combines the two. Therefore, going forward, let's consider metrics and KPIs as one and the same, as is commonly accepted, but keep them distinct from leading indicators.

Quickly taking this discussion into the arena of American football, you have great leading indicators; for example, the percentage of time in possession of the ball (the leading indicator), which helps to indicate the potential to score points (the metric). An example from the business world can be the number of requests for quotation, which is a leading indicator to potential sales (the metric). In between these, you could have an additional leading indicator, which is the win ratio of quotations, a more direct indicator of sales and a gauge of the accuracy of your quotation process versus the competition's quotation process.

The process box (the lower portion of the Post-it or split box in the Indicator-Process row) should be the vision of what major processes, programs, or steps will help the organization to reach these goals. This will be either confirmed, and then detailed at the department levels, or the catch-ball and analysis might indicate these require revising. I have encountered the best results when senior leaders are involved in this level of detail, because it requires both analysis and going to where the processes are performed for a better understanding of what may be possible. This should force you away from sitting in an ivory tower and setting goals without involving the team.

Involving the Departmental Managers

After the *top* leaders reach a consensus on the proposal for the first three rows, it is time to involve the departmental management level. Before either formal or informal discussions start happening or any catch-ball begins, it is the responsibility of the leadership to not only communicate their annual proposal, but also connect this with the longer-term goals (three to five years). And it is most important to clarify the reasons necessitating these objectives. This should include an explanation from top leadership of the customers, the market, and pertinent analysis, starting with the process of establishing the current situation. Ideally, you want awareness to drive a two-way dialogue, not just a one direction PowerPoint show. Especially during the first years of strategy deployment, you also want to outline the upcoming process steps for deployment and present a proposed timetable.

Following this sharing of information, you have options of how to proceed, but ideally you would provide time for the team to familiarize and digest what was discussed. This allows a technique to begin known as a *nemawashi* (a Japanese term for informally laying the groundwork for a proposed change by discussing and gathering support outside the formal discussions). I believe this happens to some extent in any organization (where it would likely be referred to as "laying the groundwork"), although it is good to recognize this *nemawashi* and take advantage of the benefits it offers throughout the strategy-deployment process and in other continuous improvements.

In some cases the top leadership might find a way to proportion the targets between the departments based on their analysis; for example, imagine you target a ten-day lead-time reduction between order entry and production scheduling, you might already have analysis indicating a three-day average reduction could come from sales, a four-day reduction in engineering, a two-day purchasing time reduction and finally a one-day average reduction from the production planning process. In other instances, you might want the various departments involved to come together and brainstorm how they can collectively reach the ten-day target.

As the department leaders help in completing the strategy deployment matrix (Figure 2.3, the middle and bottom sections), you are first deciding whether a quadrant is left blank or that the department can support the organization in reaching its objective (i.e. does it get a Post-it or doesn't it?). To facilitate this discussion, consider introducing the concepts *influence* and/or *control*.

Departmental leaders may be quick to point out they do not have control over a certain target. For example, as the company developed what is now in Figure 3.2, the finance manager said he was not responsible for productivity and quickly pointed out that this was mostly in operation's *control*; after further discussion, he became convinced he had an *influence* in helping break down and understand the root causes of variation, and this supports operations in better focusing their attention. So as the catch-ball occurs, when a department claims it is not responsible or in *control*, question whether the people in that department can have an *influence* on this objective. In other words, the strategy deployment matrix should be used to flush out more support for the objectives where we might have traditionally left a blank. This leads to more team improvements and world-class organizations.

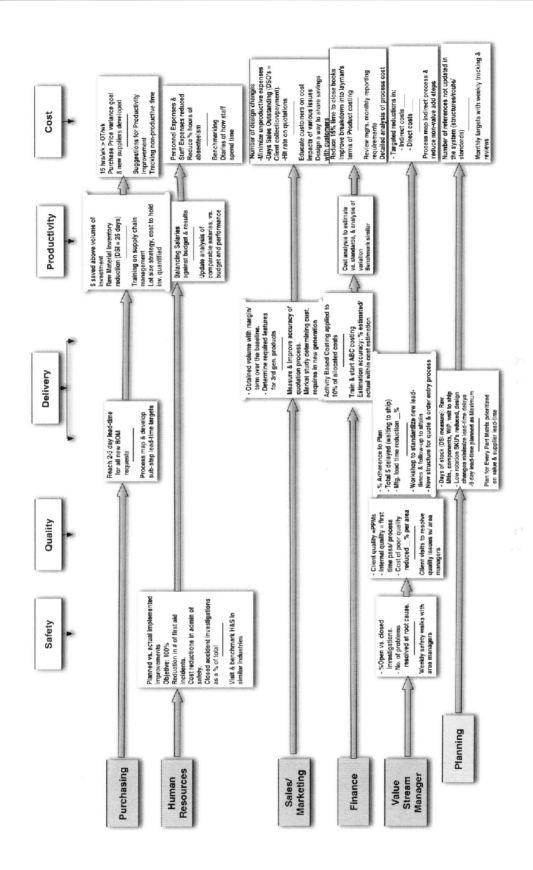

Figure 3.2: Strategy Deployment Matrix (Departmental Section)

There is no correct number of iterations for the catch-ball, there is no point where it is set in stone and everyone is so in love with the strategy that it cannot change. That's not to say you want to be unfocused, or you have no firm timetable in determining your breakthrough and continuous improvement objectives, but the scientific method has always followed the loop of hypothesis, experiment, validate, and conclusions. Therefore, you need to try something, and then validate it, and if your hypothesis is incorrect, try another hypothesis, thereby making it difficult to plan a specific time period.

You also want to avoid a fixation on immediate gratification and flavors of the month. Set both your high-level breakthrough and improvement objectives, confirm and validate these as you deploy through the various levels, by determining what processes, structures, and actions will achieve them. Then readjust the targets if you determine they cannot be met. You are analyzing and experimenting to determine where interdependencies exist between processes, actions and measurements. Then there must be a period, where you work to change structures, implement processes, and implement actions. If you are not able to confirm these actions or new processes that can attain their individual goals (which together amount to the overall objective), you must first revise these at department and team levels until you exhaust all options before giving consideration to revising any top-level objectives.

Department Managers' Involving Their Teams

The deployment does not end at the department level; it continues by separating department objectives from team-level objectives utilizing the catch-ball process. If your organization has the equivalent of team leaders, it is easier to implement the next level of formal and informal catch-ball.

At the department level, you have identified objectives, separated those into metrics, and determined processes or actions to achieve them. Now you want to take the proposed metrics and associate them with leading indicators for the team leaders, and take the departmental proposed actions and detail more specific team actions. One-way to look at both the strategy deployment matrix and the deployment process as you move through the organization's levels (top leadership, departmental leaders, team leaders) is that you are reducing the focus of your timeframe. You can think of this as moving from monthly toward weekly and finally to daily. At the weekly and daily levels, you are shifting from measurements toward indicators. You also begin breaking down high-level actions to the team and individual levels. There will be cases at the team level where you might move to hourly indicators, but that is outside the scope of this discussion.

You can think in terms of the first three rows of the strategy deployment matrix (refer to Figure 3.1), working in monthly and periodically weekly measurements. At the department levels (see Figure 3.2), try to reach weekly levels and, at the team level, have indicators in daily and hourly time frames (smaller time frames allow you to react quicker reducing the impact of the abnormality).

The same is true with the action plans. As department managers clarify the strategy deployment matrix for their team leaders (remember this is a learn it, do it, and teach it approach), they will start at the top, explaining the necessity and data behind the high level objectives (i.e. the need for change), and then they will explain the catch-ball process to arrive at the departmental measurements and actions. Finally, they will begin the catch-ball with the team leaders to verify whether detailed plans can be developed to obtain the departmental level goals, as stated in the strategy deployment matrix. These team level leading indicators and action plans will normally be displayed on a separate panel in the team area (since trying to include this level of detail on the strategy deployment matrix would make it too unwieldy). Remember when planning, however, that the devil is in the details.

If team leaders are not able to determine plans they believe can support the department's proposed objectives and actions, the department managers must return to discussions with top leadership, which could result in the top-level objectives being revised. Remember this process is not about forcing objectives, but about gaining agreement by working through the detailed processes and actions necessary to accomplish improvements, then breakthrough targets. The targets should be challenging and may push people beyond their comfort level, but they need to see them as achievable. If there is not openness toward revising objectives, you are back to a command-and-control environment and will likely be less successful. You are taking advantage of the human psyche in that, if someone helps develop a target through analysis and reflection, he or she is going to be personally committed and will go above and beyond the call of duty in attaining the objective.

You want to develop your front line team leaders to become comfortable in setting targets for process improvements. They are the ones with first hand knowledge and once they gain some experience in developing targets you have quite a power situation. Ideally this should evolve to the point they can relate their targets back upstream in terms of how they will influence revenue. You really want them to be able to develop the *business case* for the process improvements they are proposing.

Advantages of the Strategy Deployment Matrix Over Other Methodologies

Although there are many formats available in which to work through deploying your strategy (like A3 Strategy Deployment or the X-matrix that have been discussed and displayed), I find the matrix developed in both chapters 2 and 3 to be superior for the following reasons.

- Encourages top leadership to communicate the necessity for high-level objectives in relation to customers and market requirements (by including the second portion written on each Post-it in every cell of the Objectives row)

- Mixture of breakthrough and continuous improvement objectives are encouraged and distinguished

- Processes, actions, and metrics recognized at each level

- Distinguishes between metrics and leading indicators

- Involves all departments and clearly shows their focus; nobody is left to just delegate changes; everyone takes part.

- Is a living and breathing form of communication to be continuously displayed and updated, instead of a formal initiative where the focus quickly returns to day-to-day firefighting

- Creates a structure of the top leadership learning and using the strategy deployment matrix, before teaching it to the departmental level, which the department leaders then complete before teaching to the team level (the strategy deployment matrix guides this as you work from top to bottom)

Possible Links with the Strategy Deployment Matrix

This strategy deployment matrix leads to the recognition of other necessary processes and improvements associated with world class organizations, a few of those most directly linked to the matrix's development are noted.

- Where succession planning is deemed appropriate (i.e. you can indicate this by cross-hatching Post-its), you want this strategy deployment matrix linked to your skills matrix and training plans.

- Personnel performance reviews can be related with the objectives agreed to in the strategy deployment matrix.

- Departments and teams should have action plans on their boards for daily management of the tasks committed to in the strategy deployment matrix.

Briefly exploring performance reviews, which are an important element when transforming a culture, the implication is that you need to also include soft issues in each person's review (at least for the department leaders, value stream leaders, and so on). This will obviously be much more subjective then a typical performance appraisal that focuses on technical solutions, with firm objectives and quantifiable metrics. When creating the Cultural Transformation Plan (see Chapter 5), you will discuss the important link to performance reviews. In performance reviews, consider cultural changes like cost control versus cost cutting, working on both incremental improvements and supporting breakthroughs, balancing team and individual performance, and long-term versus short-term thinking. An example of how corporate America has changed its focus from short-term to long-term objectives is the trend toward stock options being given to executives only after a vested period of typically three to five years, meaning their strategies are rewarded only if they promote longer-term success for the organization.

Criticality of Follow-up on Culture Change

In a typical command-and-control environment, the review cycle becomes most important when objectives are not met. These situations are not about testing hypotheses, learning, rewarding for participation (as well as successful results), or rewarding for small (and continuous) improvements. The command and control review leaves team members only with the perception that management's sole interest is in results, where leaders should be also interested in the processes and learnings. This is what you are striving for in your changed culture, and the strategy deployment matrix should help in moving away from a command-and-control approach.

Top leadership must continuously acknowledge that the business environment is changing and translate what that means. A good leader can break globalization down as to what it means to each employee, and in today's dynamic business environments, this can even lead to strategy adjustments during the year, meaning that the strategy deployment matrix could require updating and more sessions of catch-ball. It is nice to think of making an annual plan and sticking to it (avoiding flavors of the month), but today's reality is that the dynamics of certain industries might not permit that. I am not a purist who believes a three- to five-year plan will not change, and I acknowledge in certain industries that the annual planning requires certain flexibility. If you don't agree, think of the electronics and web industries—and what a year means inside that environment.

Summary

Properly deploying the strategy deployment matrix is a big change; therefore, you need to phase it in. As discussed, this is likely a three-year process until you start feeling comfortable and attaining sustainable results. You need to work your way in; for example, not focusing too much on breakthrough objectives without getting your business fundamentals in place, and then focusing and leading success through some improvement or incremental objectives. During the first year, this might be perceived as "more stuff to do," although once you have a few successes and the organization realizes its not just about day-to-day survival, you can begin introducing breakthroughs. Again, the strategy deployment matrix should help you visualize the total number of annual objectives (i.e. the five key annual objectives shown in Figures 3.1 and 3.2) because the first mistake is including everybody's wish list and pet projects, and then it will help distinguish breakthroughs versus improvement objectives.

The strategy deployment matrix should also drive change in all areas, remember it is not about delegating and doing nothing in your own area of responsibility. You should distinguish departments that have control (or responsibility) of an objective versus ones that influence the results. I did not address the "what's in it for me?" phenomenon, but there is logical connection between the strategy deployment matrix and any recognition systems within the organization. It is more about a back-and-forth process that encourages resourcefulness, not simply allowing the cry for more resources. You are trying to connect everyone with more of a sense of purpose, recognizing that the goal is not just survival but growth. In a lean organization you want to create a no blame culture that encourages experimentation and that is what is transpiring in strategy deployment as you analyze interdependencies of strategies, processes and actions.

Having been through this process with various organizations, I encourage you to begin with professional external facilitation, for the following reasons:

- In every team, you statistically have about four percent concrete heads that, for some bizarre reason, will more openly accept suggestions from an outside expert than their own leaders or managers.

- There are a multitude of hidden agendas and pet projects that can be better disseminated by a facilitator who has no concealed agendas or emotional attachments.

- There are many intricacies and soft issues in building a strategy deployment matrix that are hard to convey in a book, and experience is worth a lot when you are in the middle of the game.

After going through the process and gaining your own experience, you can teach it yourself (learn it, do it, teach it).

Following this chapter, if you believe your organization has already done an adequate job of deploying your annual strategy, verify this by asking 5 or 10 randomly chosen associates to clarify their annual goals and explain why those actions are necessary.

CHAPTER 4

Cultural Considerations

Improving organizational cultural is the underlying focus of the methodology shared in this book. The importance of culture in an organization is exemplified in its definition: *values, norms, and traits shared within a group, resulting in predicable behavior and having an influence on decision-making*. This set of shared behaviors and traits within a culture has a strong effect on decision-making, which can make or break a company. To fully consider an organizational culture, we need to also consider what influence society's culture plays.

Society's Culture

I consider myself fortunate in regard to speaking about how a society's cultural exerts influence when transforming an organization's culture. I have been part of lean transformations in more than 30 countries during the past two decades, which has involved diverse national cultures, religions, languages, and politics. It includes working in first world countries and third world developing nations. That being said, I do not believe I have come across a culture within a country that opposes implementing a lean culture *or* improving the existing traditions to support the organization's objectives.

This is not meant to say that you can overlook a society's culture and traditions when moving toward a continuous improvement culture. Actually, each culture has traditions that complement a lean cultural and some traditions that go against the grain, but because changing society's culture is difficult and transpires over generations, take advantage of those traditions that complement lean thinking and support your mental transformation, while incorporating ideas into the company's culture to overcome traditions that impede lean thinking.

More and more, we work in multi-cultural environments in global industries within a worldwide economy; therefore, it is likely that you are dealing with a multiple of cultures in your organization. Most organizations will be left to account for the primary culture of their society when undertaking a transformation with some thought given to major influences from minority cultures working within the company.

Some change agents have visited Japanese companies that have successfully implemented improvement cultures and returned home with the belief that "their society's culture has allowed them to create their organization's culture," and because American culture is fundamentally different, they also believe we cannot recreate that type of lean culture here. I do not believe that, because I have witnessed improvement cultures created in countries where that same statement has been made. Remember that much of Japan's quality movement came from American-created methods and ideologies (from the likes of Deming and Juran), which required an organizational cultural change—and certain Japanese organizations succeeded. Whether you live in a society that starts the day with strong coffee or weak coffee, or green tea instead of gray, you need to generate respect and equity among the entire team. Naturally, there are cultures in which this is easier than others, but within any country, you have the opportunity to develop or change the organization's culture.

As I talk through developing what will become your Cultural Transformation Plan, you will find there is a point at which you are encouraged to deal with the soft issues that are influenced by the country's culture. For example, in countries of Latino origin, there is often an emotional influence in decision-making, whereas in Anglo Saxon (and especially Germanic) countries, there tends to be more analytical thinking when making a decision. This should be taken into account in Chapter 8, when you analyze where you fall on the intuitive-versus-analytical thinking scale and what actions you should consider.

You must recognize how cultures create differences that affect your operation of the business and specifically how you select and balance your team. In terms of skill sets, we know, for example, that India offers great mathematical and engineering abilities and Germany has a great apprentice program for machinists. Americans are often considered to be superior at developing new markets. Northern Europeans spend more time and effort on formal training and learning, whereas Americans jump in with Yankee ingenuity, inventive improvisations, and adaptations. These backgrounds prove true more often than not and should be taken into account when hiring, selecting teams, and creating an individual's Cultural Transformation Plan to complement your desired organizational traits and behaviors.

Organizational Culture

Organizational culture is the beliefs, behaviors, and other characteristics common to an organization that affect decision-making and are responsible for creating social and psychological environments.

Your organization culture is the difficult but crucial part of a transformation, and the one for which you can have direct impact. Let me start with a recent example of some observations and see whether you pick up on some of the key cultural impediments. Remember that throughout this example, you not only need kaizen eyes (*kaizen* in this context meaning continuous improvement) to identify opportunities on the shop floor, but also need your observations tuned to identify the soft or cultural issues.

An Example of Cultural Disconnect

Yesterday (and I mean that literally, as I sit and write this book), I went on my first visit with a potential client. The initial contact came from the general director of the organization, and the plan was to meet and discuss where they were on their continuous improvement journey, what type of support they were looking for, and what I could offer them. As I entered the director's private office, he closed the door and sat down without removing his coat or necktie. He intelligently and articulately explained the company's background, the current business environment and the problems it presented to his organization, he also conveyed his lean knowledge and his company's journey to this point, and how the "employees," as he referred to them, have responded to change. His assessment came out rapid fire, making it difficult to even squeeze in a question or apply any coaching. As we left the office to visit some other departments located within isolated areas, someone was waiting at the locked entrance doors to the office area. He held open the door with a stern look and permitted her to enter (I assume she was an "employee"), and asked where she was going that required her to enter the office area. The reply came that the bathroom was her destination, and the intrusion was allowed. As we walked through the various supporting departments (planning, purchasing, and the like) and then onto the production floor, the director explained all the processes and the improvements. During the entire five or six hours I spent there, I was lucky to squeeze in 15 minutes of questions/discussion.

Remember that the director who had invited me was the enlightened one in regard to continuous improvement. He had been brought onboard three years ago as the driving force of change and had latched on to lean as a great way to go about that. During our talk, he repeatedly referred to *cultural* problems that were historic in the company, and although he knew that those needed to be changed, he was concerned this would be a serious roadblock in their transformation, and surely he did not sense that any of his habits or beliefs required change.

The following list is what I picked up as challenges with the *director's behavior* that would impede implementing a continuous improvement culture. Most important is to always lead by example, and remember our discussion on leadership in Chapter 1; it's not what you say, but what you do.

- His title of "general director" not only implies that his job is to direct but he has other sub-levels of directors reporting to him, also responsible to direct (so they have a push system)

- Private office

- Closed door (tending to mean, "discussing secret things")

- Suit and necktie (distinguishing an us-versus-them, formality, exclusivity)

- Not listening and instead dominating the conversation (instead of allowing the consultant/advisor to utilize their coaching techniques of asking leading questions to draw someone toward a conclusion)

- Locked doors to the office (us-versus-them, mistrust, secret things)

- Separate offices (key functions not inserted into the value stream's flow), poor flow of information, and poor team work

- The boss explaining the processes and improvements (instead of team leaders and members taking pride in their processes and their improvements; not showing respect for everyone)

- Unclear purpose and expectations

- Using the managerial words, for example, "employee" instead of "associate" or "teammate"

- Very stiff and closed body language (nonverbals)

There are likely points I missed in my observation, and any of the points I identified that you overlooked are probably because you accept some of these behaviors as normal. Some of these items may seem incidental or hard to change in your existing culture, but since I have experienced that changing many of these habits are critical in realigning a culture to help in meeting its strategic objectives, let's discuss a few in more detail.

In all organizations, titles are given; many would also deem them as necessary within society or an industry. For example, in industries within the United States, titles like president and vice president are utilized; in England they use managing director or operations director to indicate that level of responsibility. Of course, legally, you need to designate a president or managing director, but whatever words you are obliged to utilize to comply with society's demands, from inside the organization, isn't it better to have various leaders and refer to them according to the specific role they fill? We want our titles to reflect the roles and responsibilities we expect in an improved culture. Take, for example, in Toyota's production areas, you have team members, team leaders, and group leaders (instead of supervisors). Again think of the connotation of the word "supervisor," which Webster's defines as "an administrative officer in charge of a business, government, or school unit or operation." That has the connotation of an enforcer, someone who pushes. You see my point. Titles are critical, and they need to be taken seriously, as well as their respective job descriptions. Although you don't want to just jump into superficially changing titles, you need to do some work behind the scenes and first rewrite the responsibilities in line with lean thinking, and then consider the appropriate name. In this book, considerable effort is invested distinguishing between a manager and a leader. Although some individuals will not be able to transition their traits and behaviors to those of a leader, it should be a focal point for your organization.

Rewriting Job Descriptions

An easy starting point for rewriting job descriptions is to obtain copies from world-class lean organizations and compare these to your respective written descriptions. This simple step might be complicated if you do not have accurate and updated job descriptions, although if that is the case, don't feel you are alone, as many organizations are in a similar situation.

I have recreated Toyota's roles and responsibilities for team leaders in some of my other books and have included it here in Appendix C as an important starting point. The reason I chose team leaders as an example is that they perform a critical role as problem solvers inside Toyota. Although some organizations believe they have someone filling a similar role as that of the team leader, they are often overlooking key responsibilities that are part of the underlying cultural and structural support issues found in transformations. Remember that it all works together as an integrated system, and cherry-picking methods or tools won't lead to sustainable results. Creating an organization of problem solvers is a key objective in your transformation, and you require structure to support this.

After rewriting job descriptions, consider what traits are necessary versus the traits of individuals currently in those roles. You need to answer this: "Is it only awareness and training that are required to align the individual with the new roles, or is going to take years to grow into this new environment?" Remember that we humans are creatures of habit and find comfort in known environments with known tasks. You are likely to determine a few cases in which a particular individual will not be able to grow into the new roles and responsibilities, and that will require you to start taking appropriate steps to either relocate or remove the person. As your work through defining the desired traits and behaviors for your cultural change, some members will not be able to adapt to the new roles and responsibilities, and this will lead to tough decisions.

Properly Communicating

Communication by its nature involves listening, but if you consider yourself the smartest or most interesting person in the room, communication is likely to become a one-way street. Now I concede that this is not only an individual trait, but in certain parts of the world, the ability to listen can be associated with the surrounding society, meaning some cultures seem to like lots of loud talking, mostly one directional, and find patient listening more difficult.

When moving toward a lean culture, you and your team need to move toward becoming leaders and mentors. In Chapter 9, we will discuss this in more detail, but for now you want to move from a push to a pull form of communication; the trick is this takes patience and often requires much more time spent listening than talking. The end result is usually well worth the time invested, however, because the mentor now has the mentee's buy-in and ownership of the idea; therefore, the mentee is likely to expel much more effort in getting the idea to work and getting others to support it. As this is a learned skill, it must be continually reinforced, but if it is not followed by those higher up in the organization—those responsible to lead cultural change—there is little hope. The first step is awareness, specifically awareness at the top of the organization. I imagine if I am to begin working with that client I visited yesterday, I need to start creating this awareness with the director, but it will be a true test of my patience as a mentor to see whether I can force enough challenging questions into the conversation to refocus his perspective.

Private Offices Restrict Open Communication

The next cultural issue to be discussed is private offices. When I worked at NUMMI (the Toyota and General Motors joint venture in California), everyone—and I mean everyone—was in open offices. Naturally, there were conference rooms available for private discussions and phone calls. And let's be honest: in open offices, there are the disadvantages of noise and distractions in these large areas, and you must consider whether the advantages outweigh the disadvantages.

I am confident they do. The improved team building, value-stream management, problem solving, and so on in open offices are well worth the extra noise and distractions, with the exceptions of some creative industries, where people need separate spaces to develop ideas. I think the hardest part to overcome in getting rid of offices, though, are our expectations and ego, true leaders tend to have small egos. Western societies associate hard work and success with the corner office and its great views, and who is not a bit susceptible to these allures? But you can't have it both ways: a democratic business (having social equality) on the one hand *and* elite treatment on the other. It will always become, "I hear what you're saying, but I see what you're doing."

A Word on Coaching

Regarding my encounter, where the director took the responsibility to explain the processes and improvements, he has implied process ownership and claimed responsibility for the improvements. Now you might be thinking he was just being polite by not interrupting the team members, or they could not afford the time as they would get behind in their work, or he was just being practical and quick. Although I don't think that is how the team members view it, overall it is not demonstrating respect, all these personal relationships should be viewed as a business asset.

Think how proud an operator is to explain some details of his/her process, if for no other reason than to break up the boredom of that job. These team members likely realize that their process is not rocket science, but it is what they do and they do it better than anyone else, and their pride shows through. (And if you're worried about work backing up, there should always be a system for that, like the team leader stepping in). Remember that a good coach questions you through the problem solving without suggesting solutions; therefore, those solutions become "your" solutions, and you should be the one sharing those with visitors. In the case of yesterday's shop floor walk, it's likely there are deeper issues and the improvement ideas are actually coming from the management in a top-down command-and-control style instead of from the entire organization.

This is just one example of problems with the organizational culture in a medium-size business, but in this case, it is crucial that the same enlightened person who is trying to lead the change (who is also readily pointing out that the organization is bureaucratic and will be difficult to change because of the company's age and complicated history) doesn't realize he is not leading by example and is more a part of the problem than the solution. Therefore, an initial step in a transformation is to outline what traits and behaviors are desirable in the new culture, as explained in Chapter 5.

Although it many seem this cultural change is insurmountable, the good news is you need only a few at the top of the organization to create the right philosophy, by coaching and mentoring each day. The notion of "become one, generate one" comes to mind in terms of coaching.

The importance of coaching has been long established, although more recently you can find significant reinforcement of its successes from Training Within Industry (TWI). This was a U.S. organized service from 1940 to 1945 that assisted war production in meeting demands of manpower and output during World War II. This highly successful effort of increasing output during the war (also the basis of contemporary lean manufacturing), cited *coaching* as a greatly improved method for the supervisor to interact with his team. Although TWI worked to improve productivity for badly needed war supplies by focusing on supporting the supervisor to be a better trainer, coaching was cited as one of the driving factors in increasing productivity and reducing grievances. This is demonstrated in TWI's data report from the War Production Board's account from September 1945 (see Appendix F).

From my own experience buying and transforming a small manufacturing company, I was a believer in coaching and leadership, and since I was at the top of my small domain, I worked each day to refine my coaching skills in hopes that it led others toward improving their coaching abilities. In retrospect, not being a patient person, I am sure there were more times then I care to think where I directed someone instead of having led them to a their own conclusions. But this is why the Cultural Transformation Plan starts at the top with awareness and self-reflection, because if you get it working at the top, it will spread throughout the organization.

Summary

The habits and traits of society must be taken into account in your transformation, but this will not block your organization's cultural change. Since you cannot change society's ingrained habits, you need to exploit those traits that are in line with the desired organizational culture and incorporate proactive steps in your Cultural Transformation Plan to overcome the disadvantages created by society's customs that might keep you from reaching your transformation's objectives.

On the other hand, the organization's culture is where you can effect change, no matter how difficult or slow it may be. Therefore, the thrust of the Cultural Transformation Plan put forth in this book focuses on the organization's culture, including how to create awareness and what proven actions can attain tangible results.

CHAPTER 5

Your Cultural Transformation Plan

A Cultural Transformation Plan is a developmental process to create self-awareness of leadership's mindsets, and compare that awareness to the desired traits and behaviors that lead to reaching breakthrough objects. It is a comprehensive plan to develop the soft issue's for your most valuable assets, your team's capabilities, and will complement any existing plans to develop their hard skills. This manifests itself in an action plan. While 56% of manufacturers surveyed had some type of 'human-capital' management (soft skill focus), only 13% of those indicated they had full engagement and buy-in to those plans.[23]

Most organizations are already working to some degree on changing traits and behaviors, but it is rarely a comprehensive plan or well linked to the strategy. For example, you might have a need for new team leaders and create a developmental training model that will also address soft skills, but this might be limited to only those being trained for the team leader role. The Cultural Transformation Plan being discussed has some fundamental differences to some of the plans you might have in place; it's comprehensive, it involves engaging all levels and teams, and to ensure real change it encourages non-biased self-awareness of existing behaviors, instead of assuming change can be pushed onto the team.

The plan being presented here also differs from those devised for organizations that have reached a critical stage (i.e. having a 'burning platform'). Take for example famous cases like Alcoa, when Paul O'Neill was brought in to turn the tide on their problems. When a new CEO is appointed and brings new habits and styles, this approach differs from what an existing management team must undergo to change behaviors and habits in support of their strategic objectives. This book focuses on changing behaviors within the current leadership by identifying necessary behaviors to succeed and creating individual awareness of the current state of these *soft* issues.

Deploying a long-term strategy relies on communicating the technical and tangible matters, although to extract these to the best of the organization's abilities, you must address the soft side of cultural change. Addressing these behavioral traits is also necessary in obtaining your longer-term strategic objectives. Many managers have technical or professional backgrounds and have advanced based on either work they've personally done or by applying their own expertise.

Remember that the more you assume responsibility for leading strategic change, the more you require interpersonal skills, because organizational improvement is achieved by leading others. *Leadership is the key to cultural change.* This awareness of the necessity for a balance between technical and soft skills proves itself in today's dynamic world, as "adult learners constitute a growing percentage of enrolled students."[5] A significant portion of this increase in adult education is taking place within leadership classes.

In this chapter, we move our focus to the second major step in supporting the strategic objectives: developing the Cultural Transformation Plan. We are moving into what I call the *soft* issues, and although this involves beliefs, traits, behaviors, and mindsets, there is a pragmatic way to work through identifying and implementing soft-issue improvements.

Taking the time to develop detailed plans covering the who, what, when, and how you're going to accomplish improvement, leads to higher levels of success; in this case, catchball is utilized to increase ownership and follow-up. In addition, this visible Cultural Transformation Plan demonstrates respect for the team, knowing that the plan allows them to realize and reach their full potential. A good analogy is the hard (technical) skills are the portion of an iceberg we see above the surface, and the soft skills are the portion of the iceberg hiding under the water and posing the most danger. Making a conscious effort to also address these soft skills is one way to expose their impact.

Other common wordings for an Cultural Transformation Plan might be a lean transformation, where you are changing the organization's culture to support a more viable business defined through the strategy deployment. This is all about thinking and acting differently, which sure is easy to put into words, but requires dedication and support from all associates. It involves successfully changing your mindset to reach breakthrough objectives, which is a tall order. You obviously need to make some kind of a transformation in your culture in at least part of the organization—purists would say the *entire* organization, but the majority ride the fence and will follow the momentum, and only about four percent will actively resist transformations. So the odds are in your favor. Admitting that there are personal traits and behaviors (i.e. parts of the culture) that require change is an important step, although you can be even more successful by working as a team to create awareness and commitment to this in a PDCA type format.

Note: You can consider the Cultural Transformation Plan to be for the *'soft'* issues what a cross training matrix (or skills matrix) is for the hard (technical) issues. It is a developmental process to plan where you have shortcomings in your behaviors with regard to attaining your objectives. The cross training matrix on the other hand identifies where you have skills shortages in your technical (or job related) requirements.

Quantifying Resistance to Change

Although Toyota's data demonstrates that two to four percent of the workforce proactively develops ideas and encourages change and another two to four percent[6] actively resist change, in the United States, there is some additional data to consider: a recent Gallop poll of almost 32,000 workers found that 18 percent are "actively disengaged;"[7] these are naysayers who like to complain about their employers. When considering improvement and developing a Cultural Transformation Plan, be sure to consider this group, as they can have an effect on productivity and can derail improvement. If you sum up these two groups (4 percent resisting change +18 percent of actively disengaged whiners), the resulting 22 percent can be overcome with a plan.

But that 22 percent can expand if you are not careful, so consider ways in which you can educate the remaining workforce to minimize the effect. These include asking the whiner what he or she intends to do about it (i.e. confronting the person with whom you have an issue) or isolating the whiner so they cannot distract and reduce the effectiveness of others. Do not, however, completely overlook criticisms, as some of these complaints expose real problems and can be constructive if approached in the right manner. For example, you might consider a time allotment in meetings for constructive discussion regarding negative interactions.

That being said, in approaching the transformation toward meeting your strategic objectives, focus on the three quarters of the team who are riding the fence, so to speak, instead of investing your leadership's energy in converting the disengaged. My experience is that the majority wins out, and you are better identifying where you have willingness to realign your behaviors.

Your annual personnel performance evaluations (assuming you have a structured system in place) are also a good indicator of where you might encounter resistance. Normally when a person's goals are determined for the next year they will include a mix of more tangible objectives and possibly a few behaviors or traits to work on improving. The success the team member experiences in altering any behaviors is a good indication of whether a supportive environment exists, as it is difficult to alter behaviors without the support of those around you. These annual performance evaluations can also play a key part in how to deploy some of the traits and behaviors you acknowledged as requiring change (as you build your Cultural Transformation Plan).

Note: Since people don't resist change as much as they resist being changed, an approach Toyota utilized in their personnel performance evaluations was to have the person being evaluated propose their own objectives for the upcoming year, instead of their manager handling this. Although these were then reviewed and possibly altered by the manager, it provided the opportunity for reflection and potentially more buy-in. It also allows the leader to better understand his or her team members thinking and where they see the need for change.

Defining Mentality

Mentality is defined as a habitual or characteristic mindset that determines how you will interpret and respond to a situation;[8] naturally, this is a crucial element to address in any transformation as well as in life. Your mentality takes shape all during your life as you go through your experiences; therefore, a change is difficult, to say the least, but it happens all the time. As this will be a big change you need to start with non-biased self-awareness of how your current mentality affects decision-making in reaching breakthrough objectives. Remember most of us are proud of our mentality, however, and feel it is superior, so creating a reason for change is probably the biggest challenge. You can consider that certain habits will need to be altered and to accomplish this you need to address the craving that leads to the reward (reshaping habits will be discussed in chapter 7).

An interesting exercise to see how differently your organization thinks, and better recognize that we should consider those differences is to ask your team to privately write their answers to each of the following questions. Then facilitate the team in listing their range of answers and grasp how large the multiplier is between the largest and smallest values provided.

- There are lots of people in line. How many people are there?

- The store is far away. How many miles to the store?

- Luxury cars are expensive. How much does one cost?

- A lot of errors were encountered. How many errors were experienced?

- The box is heavy. How many pounds does the box weigh?

Where the team arrives at a multiplier of say 40X or 100X between responses, they need to both appreciate the difference in people's perceptions, and understand how it can affect traits and behaviors.

Using the word "cultural" before "transformation" infers we need to change our mentality, and to change what's between someone's ears, which has been devolving since early childhood, is a tall order, but it transpires daily throughout the world. Chapter 1 established that the majority of lean (cultural) transformations fail because the culture was not able to change, and knowing the culture change is driven by the mentality of the leadership, you can only imagine how critical and complicated this is. Taking Toyota as an example, many are surprised by how open they have made their operational areas to public visits, often including visits by direct competitors. In theory, they are sharing the Toyota Production System (their secret weapon) and answering all questions openly, often explaining the detailed inter-workings of their tools like kanban, Andon , heijunka, and so on. Even tour groups that include people advanced in their understanding of the cultural necessities required for success, when asking questions about soft issues, find the answers difficult to act on. Therefore Toyota is a bit smug in knowing continuous improvement culture is really their secret weapon and few will be able to change what is deeply embedded in their cultures. Many of us have studied or read about companies like Wiremold (explored and exposed by J. Womack and D. Jones as a successful example) and Danaher (with the Danaher business system), some of the more prominent examples of successfully sustaining a cultural transformation. But they are a minority.

In short, I am going to walk you through a successful technique for making headway with cultural change, demonstrated through actual examples. Naturally, this is a learning process and is not rigid or fixed but in a constant state of development. There are basic steps to follow:

- Awareness

- Analysis of current and desired culture at the organizational level

- Identifying desired traits to support the strategy at the value stream level

- Individual awareness of current traits and behaviors

- Individuals engaging in the development of action plans to foster the desired traits

- Execution

- Follow-up

Details within each step that have proven successful are of the most value. The idea is to create awareness in your leadership (ideally going from top down) of each leader's own mentality as it applies to decision-making in dealing with specific situations. This will involve self-assessments to start creating awareness of the current state. After some additional analysis, you will work to build a Cultural Transformation Plan; ideally, this is done on an individual *leader's* level. The methodology helps ensure you keep this on a professional and not a personal level, because the mentality changes required can become a touchy subject. Can you imagine telling your spouse that you want him or her to work on changing his or her mentality?

For those who are uncomfortable sharing their self-assessments and displaying their personal transformation plan, we can fall back to a more general transformation plan where desired traits are identified for each position, but plans to alter that individual's current behaviors are not documented. I encourage you to be bold and work toward individual plans that are documented, as this achieves better results. Acceptance has a lot to do with the way in which you involve the team and how you communicate the necessity of transforming the mentality.

I hope you see the strong link between strategy deployment and the need to transform mentalities in the organization. To successfully deploy a strategy that includes breakthrough objectives, as discussed in Chapter 3, you likely have some changes to make in the organization's culture. This is why the strategy deployment and Cultural Transformation Plan are displayed side by side in Figure 2.1 (see Chapter 2). It also brings us back to considering the sequence in which these plans should be developed: and the simple answer is, "it depends on the situation and the organization." Neither the strategy deployment nor the Cultural Transformation Plan are short or simple projects, but the strategy deployment should result in increased earnings along with highlighting the need to transform the culture (to help in meeting those objectives). So unless you find yourself in a rare and unique situation, first get your strategy in order, and then change the traits and behaviors to support the strategy. My experience confirms that the reason for any cultural change is to achieve the desired strategic objectives; therefore, I will proceed, assuming you need to justify any social change with a deliberate business reason—that is, strategy first, and then the cultural change to support it.

In the normal course of events, when implementing strategy deployment, the ingrained organizational culture becomes highlighted as a blocker and increases the awareness of the need for change. This culture is not documented; it is intangible but always there in the background as the basis of our actions.

How Cultural Change Succeeds

So for a head-on approach like this, instead of just talking in general terms about creating leadership and changing the organization's culture, let's first explore what you are attempting to overcome. It entails:

- A future in which most will be happy

- A result worth the investment and effort

- Focused and achievable results without becoming personal

- Flexibility maintained through reviews and revisions

- Top leadership that better understands human behaviors, habits, cultural change, and social mentality

- Change leadership and changing organizational culture

- Creating a burning platform and sense of urgency without insulting people's current mentalities

The plan needs to address resistance, which comes from:

- Our state of mind and our norms

- Complacency

- Fear of the unknown

- Fear of change

- Habits

- Risk to our careers

Making a cultural transformation requires you to have courage and humility, and this is best accomplished by senior leaders first going through some of the recommended self-assessments and leading with their own transformations in mentalities, imagining how *leading by example* will open up the other team members. It is important that you do not utilize *evaluations* (meaning that someone *evaluates* someone else) in the context of this professional development; evaluations are associated with bureaucratic organizations. You want only to create awareness by leaders completing self-assessments; this leads to collective inquiry, reflection, and the shared norms you want in a professional organization. More bureaucratic organizations might attempt cultural change with more formal evaluations being reported back through the hierarchy with the expectation of changing certain traits or behaviors.

Courage is also required in assuming the advantages of this change will outweigh the disadvantages associated with the hard work required. A cultural change requires leaders to improve their understanding of both human and group behaviors and how they can influence them. We live in an age of easy communication but increased isolation as email and text become our predominate means of contact. Our transformation must take into account all these dynamics when trying to reach organizational goals that necessitate teamwork instead of the isolation that modern communication is driving us toward. Most successful transformations also included changes to: the organizational structure, the processes, and control methods. How and where this fits in with your Cultural Transformation Plan will depend on which stage you find yourself in.

It has been demonstrated that it is easier to stop doing something or alter a habit than to adapt a new behavior; therefore, in the pragmatic context of this book, while analyzing your various behaviors and traits, if you identify one which conflicts with the objectives desired in your new culture, it is recommended your first priority is to try and alter the routine towards a different outcome or stop doing whatever it is that is not supportive of the objectives. A second priority will be to adapt any necessary new behaviors that support the new cultural objectives you have identified. Part of the reason you will be encouraged to work as a team developing the Cultural Transformation Plan is that often you can help each other in correcting a behavior or changing a habit not in line with the desired cultural change. Self-correction combined with select colleagues or a coach helping remind you of the agreed changes will increase the chances of success.

How Cultural Change Can Fail

Few managers have more than a vague notion of the day-to-day activities required to implement a cultural change, and even fewer can sustain it. Surveys demonstrate that failing to establish a sense of urgency for change is often the reason for failure. Mistakes often start when the top *managers* (those that have not transitioned to become *leaders*) do not take into account, do not understand, or believe they should not bother with team member's assumptions, empathy is a critical behavior required for true leadership. Lacking empathy causes the team to feel unsafe or threatened. It is not easy to continuously identify and notice human behaviors, and most managers overlook its importance. Remember that most managers are much more comfortable working on technical problems instead of dealing with soft issues. Few realize how important the first words are when speaking with a colleague: how we start a conversation over an observation determines whether you assume responsibility or encourage ownership and involvement by the questions you ask.

Toyota's awareness of this infatuation with technical solutions is captured in its rarely published improvement methodology abbreviated by the acronym OSKKK, a methodology for improving any process and discourages technical solutions as the first step of improvement since they require more investment and typically have less payback. OSKKK is a form of the PDCA (Plan Do Check Act) cycle. The steps in this process are:

- Observe deeply

- Standardize (in some cases you might first need to Stabilize)

- Kaizen of the flow and process

- Kaizen of equipment

- Kaizen of layout

Although these steps are sequential, they should be viewed as a never-ending loop; once the kaizen's (continuous improvement) first cycle is completed, then observation and standardization will again be required.

The first steps of OSKKK appear as common sense, which they are, although often after only short observation periods, we "impatient problem solvers" already know the root cause and jump directly to solutions (using this intuitive instead of analytical approach is discussed in more detail in Chapter 8). Instead, we should be asking questions during this observation to begin humbly learning and involving the process owner. We know standardization is the basis from which to improve, but often the process lacks the stability to follow a standardized methodology. In this case we must first eliminate the instabilities and then try to put in place a standard process. The kaizen (continuous improvement) steps within OSKKK are in the order of effectiveness and are sorted from least to most costly to implement and in inverted order of payback on investment, meaning that kaizening the flow and process will likely have the highest payback (as you are investing only your time), while changing the layout will proportionally have less payback.

The conflict with this kaizen sequence (improve process and flow, and then improve equipment, and finally improve the layout) is that it works against human nature. It is often more tangible, exciting, and comfortable to either work on layout issues or address equipment improvements (the technical solutions) than it is to tackle process and flow issues, which normally involve traits and behaviors that are dominated by either years of using the same method, conflicting opinions, mediocre buy-in, or a general sense of comfort with the way it has always been performed.

In command-and-control style environments, it is frequently only after "confrontational" or uncomfortable questioning that the effectiveness of the existing processes can be improved; remember that all of the existing processes have a bit of personal ownership. Many of our processes are not standardized or continuously improved, but instead have evolved with the people filling those roles and are based on their talents and background (this is especially true for indirect and administrative processes). Coaching is a key skill required during all phases of OSKKK, so questions are presented in a fashion that involves the process owners instead of causing discomfort; this will be discussed as a critical step in your cultural transformation. A more detailed description of each step within OSKKK is shown in Appendix D.

When listening to top leadership in an organization, time and time again, they appear confident the organization understands what excellence means and is moving in that direction. But when speaking with team members, the perception is usually quite different. Team members vaguely recall some of the communications (speeches and written formats), although most are at a loss to explain how this change translates into their day-to-day lives. Most often, they hear what has been said (that is, what was pushed onto them), but since actions speak louder than words, they observe that the daily demands still take precedence. If you are properly and diligently working through strategy deployment, your organization better understands how each team is affected and what the expectations are.

The importance of socialization with co-workers to satisfy our human needs is something you cannot forget when developing your Cultural Transformation Plan. You must also except diversity in your organization's mentalities and plan to use that to your advantage. Keep in mind that creating a Cultural Transformation Plan has nothing to do with creating like-minded mentalities; rather, it has to do with personal awareness of our strengths and a plan to change the bad behaviors that do not support the organization's objectives. This is why it is important that you view the transformation as a personal plan that depends on:

- Where the self-assessments place your various traits and behaviors

- The parts of the assessment you agree are correct

- Which traits and/or behaviors you (and the leadership team) see as important and feasible to change

Naturally, to begin, you must have at least a few enlightened leaders to identify the need for a cultural change. If your top leaders are not reflective or introspective, if they discourage any authentic feedback, failure is likely. If leaders are either too busy to reflect on their behaviors or are not in the habit of admitting weaknesses or mistakes, it will be difficult for them to change any behaviors. Many feel that a company's success is based on their current leadership style and behaviors, so convincing them to change anything they feel has contributed to their present accomplishments can be difficult.

How to Create Awareness

Many of us deceive ourselves about the value we contribute to an organization, and this trait can complicate the need to change. We may believe our traits and behaviors have led to our accomplishments and supported the organization's accomplishments. Now your organization must grasp that to reach your breakthrough objectives, some behavioral changes are required, and your company has options in how this can be accomplished. Imagine if you had the opportunity to visit or work within another organization's culture; you could likely better grasp the advantages and disadvantages within your company's culture—and identify your bad behaviors—much more easily than if you have not experienced this external perspective. But since this is unlikely and this book does not include management shake-ups in response to a crisis, I now discuss other possibilities to create an acknowledgment of the need for change.

During the development of your strategy deployment matrix, you should drive top leadership to communicate the customer and market necessities that justify the requirement for breakthroughs. Now you are linking those required changes to the necessary behavioral changes to accomplish them. Creating additional awareness through the suggestions in the following sections further enforces additional reasons to change, allowing you to create a Cultural Transformation Plan.

Feedback Analysis

A personal and private way to increase your awareness (although more long-term) is called *feedback analysis.* A German created it sometime in the 14th century, and today it still provides a simple way to discover your strengths and weaknesses as applied to making decisions. Whenever you make a key decision, or undertake an important action, write down your expectation. Later (six months or one year) compare the actual results with what you expected (your hypothesis) and see what you can learn about yourself related to decision-making. It should demonstrate where your strengths and weakness lie in your judgments . . . and you are likely to be surprised! This approach can also help in determining whether you are better with technical decisions and actions or the human side (soft issues), and how well you can predict what will happen when there is more influence from the human side.

If you continue to practice this over a few years, it becomes a self-assessment in which you will have confidence, especially knowing that identifying where you are strong in decision-making determines the role in which you are most valuable to the organization. Focus on your strengths and ensure that your position in the organization, as well as your career path, are aligned in utilizing those strengths as well as building on them. If you are not in a position where you are making the most of these strengths, discuss this with your leader based on data from your feedback analysis.

You will also learn your weaknesses and can evaluate those against the needs of the organization and against your personal career ambitions. Once you determine where and how much effort you want to invest, you may determine that further analysis is required or start identifying an improvement plan. In short, you are moving toward your Cultural Transformation Plan, and the remainder of this book will help provide ideas of the analysis phase, as well as planning how to improve. I am a firm believer that weaknesses can be improved, and I have observed these improvements in myself and others. Not miraculous cultural transformations, but fundamental changes in human skills and each person's mindset.

Some weaknesses are also caused by shortfalls of knowledge or experience, and these are easier to resolve. These requirements should be identified and evaluated as to how the training or experience might be acquired and whether the organization is willing and able to support obtaining this experience. The best way to visualize this is on a cross-training matrix at the organizational or departmental level. (These are also referred to as skills or proficiency matrices.) I have examples of easy ways to visualize this in my book, *Made to Order Lean.*[9]

Hands-On Workshops

Another realistic way to gain a different perspective is through hands-on workshops. Some of the available training courses (training within industry) that are recommended in this phase are:

- Coaching training

- Leadership training

- Effective communication

- Standard work for managers training

- Change agent skills training (including conflict management)

- Paradigm training

- Conflict leadership training

- A3 Problem Solving training

- Job relations training

- Specific lean tools training (i.e. value-stream mapping, problem solving)

- Strategy deployment training

Develop a personalized awareness segment to determine who requires which training, instead of starting to train everyone on everything. Naturally the training, assuming it is practical, high-quality, and hands-on, will have many additional benefits for your organization. Depending on the number of people you decide will benefit from a specified training, you might find it more cost effective to hold in-house instead of external classes. Also, always follow up the training with a brainstorming session about the implications, as applied to your cultural transformation. In the beginning, the need for this training can also be identified through the self-assessments discussed in Chapter 6, although it is critical any training is linked to the overall Cultural Transformation Plan, otherwise you only create small pockets of improvement that rarely help accomplish breakthrough objectives.

Book Reviews

Creating a resource of various periodicals with topical stories about either successful leaders or organizational cultures, or those that failed to keep pace with dynamic and changing environments and did not survive can also be advantageous. Books like the one you are reading can be shared with the team and reviewed/brainstormed chapter by chapter. Also focusing on stories that demonstrate CEO behaviors that worked well in the past but did not recognize present market or environment changes and led to their downfall should be shared. You even have the extreme cases of CEO ego that didn't allow them to admit failure, leading to cheating or cooking the books; there are many stores similar to Enron's[10] that can be learning experiences. By having these stories available and asking the leadership to read and attend a type of book review can be helpful in creating awareness.

Awareness of Psychological Make-up

A final suggestion to create awareness of the opportunities toward changing your culture is to become more aware of the psychological make-up of the various team members. There are various psychological assessment tools that evaluate various parts of our mindset as applied to decisions and behaviors. Often utilizing the word *psychological* can have adverse connotations; therefore, you might refer to these as personality questionnaires. Although some might use these assessments only to create awareness, I think of them more as a step in the analysis phase of determining your personal attributes, which can then be compared to desired organizational attributes. Therefore, I propose simple psychological and behavioral self-assessments as a method to create a personalized awareness. I want to continue and reinforce that I am not saying anyone has a problem with their mentality, but that the organizational culture is a combination of its current mentalities, and mindsets must change to keep pace with our dynamic and global markets.

Summary

There is no magical solution to offer an organization in creating awareness of the need to change. Various attempts to erect and communicate a burning platform have been made, but it is best if this develops from the inside-out. This has to be instilled in the minds of the top leadership, and they need to come to terms with what is really involved on a personal and organizational level, although steps can be taken to encourage self-awareness throughout the organization.

Some of the recommendations made in this chapter that allow team members to individually explore and become conscious of the need to continuously change include:

- Hands-on training and simulations (internal and external)

- Feedback analysis (your written hypothesis versus actual results of decision making)

- Personality questionnaires (psychological self-assessments)

- Resource of periodicals (with team book/article reviews)

CHAPTER 6

Analyzing Your Current Culture and Defining Your Desired Culture

First it is best to determine where you are heading culturally with soft issues; these will be referred to as our desired traits and behaviors (others might describe them as your norms or values). A clear strategy is a key part in shaping your desired culture, so if you have already begun to implement appropriate strategy deployment, you are working through the first crucial step in creating a new culture.

Once you have transparent strategic objectives, you should begin to understand and define your existing culture. A culture is something that develops and changes to cope with the existing environment. You must now change to cope with the new environment (or your breakthrough objectives), which are often more global in nature. The success of the organization as well as that of the leader greatly depends on understanding the organization's culture. Many failures with transformations arise from failures to understand (partially through analysis) the existing culture. You should consider what a culture consists of to help in defining your current one. Some of the concepts that constitute what defines an organization's culture are listed.

The reality is this can be a difficult step, and in some organizations we have struggled and decided to bypass this step and still achieved successful results in cultural change. Most improvement methods begin with grasping the current situation and although that is what this stage is about, you are attempting it at an organizational level, although the culture is comprised of many individual traits, behaviors and habits, which are typically derived from the many subcultures. If you find difficulty in defining the organization or plant level culture, this technique goes on to its most important element, engaging each individual leader in the value streams to assess their own traits and behaviors (their individual current state) and compare those to the desired behaviors for that particular responsibility (i.e. future state), so you are still going to perform this step, although on a more personal and individual level. I recommend first trying it at the organizational level, before moving to the value stream and positional levels.

Concepts Defining an Organization's Culture

If you are going to understand your current culture as the basis for determining what behaviors must change to improve your decision-making (which ultimately results in reaching your break-through objectives), you must first understand what comprises your organization's culture.

- Traits and behaviors

- Assumptions and beliefs

- Values and norms (habits)

- Language utilized (not national language but organizational language)

- Rituals and customs

- Socialization and sub-socialization

- How problem solving is handled

- Tools and technology utilized

- Layout of work areas

How to Analyze Current Culture

Methodologies to analyze the existing culture are not rigid or well defined, although you can start with the previous list or create your own list of what you feel defines your organization's culture, and then for each area write down the way those factors manifest themselves in your company. You can also consider the presence of the commonly accepted 'bad' behaviors like: big egos, no trust, lack of curiosity, dishonestly, hiding problems, lacking follow-up, to name a few. You could try creating another column for how those concepts might manifest themselves inside your competitors or within your market's environment.

This is not easy, as some of these traits are less visible and can't be observed. Let's start with visible behavioral patterns, for example, executive perks, dress codes, and workspace layouts. Interpreting how these effect a culture and whether they have a positive or negative influence is easier than many of the soft issues. Let's explore executive perks and compare those visible in some companies versus Toyota. At Toyota plants everyone, including the top leadership, wears the same type of polo shirts (not required but encouraged), there is no special parking, everyone is treated to first come first served, and the leaders have their desks in open work areas with the rest of the team members. Think about the effect on culture when compared with an environment in which leadership wears neckties, has executive parking, and spends the day in a private corner office with a view.

Other easy observations are the words utilized by leaders and team members. They might use words to inspire, persuade, and motivate or they might bluntly use negative words that are unmotivating, can cause anger and confusion. We all have examples of when we or others have chosen the wrong word, but when assessing the culture, you are not looking for exceptions, but regular use of negative terms that do not define a successful culture. For example, if leadership refers to people in the organization as team members, associates, partners, or colleagues, they are showing respect for everyone; if, on the other hand, they use words like employees, subordinates, or workers, it signals disrespect and inequality. This is an area of observation when analyzing the current culture. More detail and examples are provided in Chapter 9, as changing vocabulary requires changing habits, and this will likely become part of your Cultural Transformation Plan.

The obvious and more visible characteristics of the culture are easier to evaluate. Although you can't "see" values and beliefs, you do understand them, like bad habits that must change to meet your strategic objectives. I feel there are generally two sets of values: the ones posted on the lobby walls with fancy words and those underlying values that really determine behavior.

In most cases, the behavior is visible, but what drives that behavior requires a bit of analysis. In this case, I would follow the theory "what is important to the boss, is important to the others" as you analyze the existing culture. One approach can be to think of how a new employee integrates into the organizational culture; it involves perceiving, evaluating, acting, and maybe believing in its importance. This kind of thinking can help you form a method to come to terms with the parts of the culture that cannot be seen. Remember that an organization's values are the cornerstones and, from there, people develop underlying assumptions to support those values, and finally those taken-for-granted assumptions form the habits and culture that many live with. Often times, even the leaders struggle to explain the culture's origins.

Subcultures within a Culture

Another critical piece of the puzzle in analyzing the existing customs is to look at the organization's cultures and *subcultures,* as there are various cultural units within an organization. Within medium or large organizations, there are groups that make up cultural entities, and they basically own that culture; therefore, you have many various subcultures operating in parallel. Some cultural entities might be discernable while others are not; it is important to truly understand

and try to identify as many of the cultural and subcultural entities as possible. Whether the culture or subculture came first and the other is a derivative is interesting to try and understand, but it may be too difficult to determine. Try listing the cultures and any subcultures you can identify and then compare these to your colleagues list (which should be developed in isolation).

Associating organizational culture with socializing and/or a social life can be another part in analyzing and understanding it. This follows from the cultural and subcultural entities within the business, so try to determine whether these groups naturally emerged out of the human need for socialization or whether naturally occurring social interactions led to these subcultures. Let me clarify this with an example, people might like to go to certain meetings to cross the paths of colleagues with whom they have some type of connection, and this creates a certain meeting culture where the issues to be resolved might be only a pretense for the meeting. Again when trying to analyze the existing culture (as a baseline toward defining the new culture), this should be considered.

You might even find departments that have evolved into their own culture of isolation by the habits to which they have become accustomed, for example communicating only with email and text. This isolation instead of teamwork is becoming a common phenomenon that needs to be taken into account when assessing the existing cultures and subcultures, versus your desired culture.

One final note: there are instruments available like the Competing Values Instrument (CVI) that measure an organization's current culture. The CVI, for example, quantifies your culture among four cultural values (clan, adhocracy, hierarchical, market). This is an inexpensive instrument and can complement the analysis suggested to this point in determining your current culture.

You may want to visualize these cultures and subcultures in a diagram and note each of their behaviors, values, and norms. These existing values can then be compared to your desired values and behaviors, to help in devising a plan.

Identifying Habits that Hold You Back

The soft issues you are attempting to identify as ideal for your new culture have nothing to do with a lack of skill or intelligence. The bad habits in your leadership team are also not due to personality flaws that require physiological evaluation. Instead, we are dealing with challenges in interpersonal traits and behaviors.

Marshall Goldsmith[11] compiled a list of 20 bad habits, some of which are more obvious than others. The partial list of bad habits that follows was recognized by Goldsmith and can be used as basis for identifying the contrary behaviors desired in your new culture:

- Winning too much. To win at all costs.

- Adding too much value. The overwhelming desire to always add your two cents.

- Passing judgment. The need to rate others and impose our standards on them.

- Making destructive comments. Needless sarcasm that we feel makes us sound witty.

- Telling the world how smart we are.

- Speaking when angry. Using emotional volatility as a leadership tool.

- Negativity. Sharing our negative thoughts even though we haven't been asked.

- Withholding information. Not sharing information so you can maintain an advantage over someone

- Failing to give recognition.

- Not listening.

- Passing the buck. The need to blame everyone but ourselves.

If you recognize some of those traits in yourself or your organization, you should prioritize which ones are most contrary to reaching your breakthrough objectives. Then the opposing good behavior (to that bad habit) should be listed as a desired trait for your new culture. You might even immediately start jotting down your opposing lists.

Many bad habits manifest themselves as wastes, which have a built-in feel-good factor, therefore they are a psychological asset and often part of the culture. Take, for example, a predominant waste that stems from people's need to stay busy, almost *wanting* to feel over-worked. The *cue* is when they sit idle with nothing to do, the *routine* is to slowly do some non-value added activity to look busy and the *reward* is not being poorly judged by your boss or team mates. This typically leads to overproduction, which is the worst waste, as all other applicable wastes are incurred during the overproduction. This overproduction does not have to be in the form of a physical product such as work in process or finished goods; it also takes place in most transactional processes, like when you batch process order entries, or order ahead to reduce the quantity of written purchase orders to a supplier, or pre-schedule weeks in advance, all with the sole purpose of staying busy. Try to identify whether this is predominant in your company's culture. The solutions include identifying slow periods in individual workloads, during which cross training and continuous improvement should be encouraged to utilize the time productively, instead of trying to look or stay busy, often causing rework when things change.

Over-processing is another waste prevalent in some cultures and related to overproduction, as it is also a stay-busy activity. This is most often observed where there are not specific or technical endpoints defined. It is also the result of not resolving problems at their root cause and instead putting in double or triple checks in an attempt to *inspect-in quality* rather than *build-in quality*. On the shop floor, over-processing can manifest itself in sanding unnecessary surfaces, or oversanding to achieve a quality finish (when a specific finish is not defined). In the office, it is often demonstrated when too much and/or unnecessary information is passed onto the next process. All this keeps you busy and creates a feeling of control and satisfaction.

Remember that, in a business, you need to reduce the difference (cost) between the inputs and outputs of all processes. Its not about hideously exceeding customer expectations; its about meeting customer expectations. Over-processing can also be used in both service and manufacturing sectors to hide unbalanced seasonal workloads. Is this prevalent in your culture? You need an open and honest culture where people feel a sense of job security if you want their help in identifying over-processing. This was re-enforced in Chapter 3 when recommending that every organization's strategy deployment must contain one high-level growth objective, so that people are encouraged to expose waste and are not fearful of improvements that could result in their jobs disappearing.

Wasteful processes and environments have costs other than poor productivity; they also provide no sense of objectives and are usually contrary to management's direction and goals. They create acceptance and reduce proactive thinking; therefore, it is critical to identify whether they are prevalent in the existing culture. Again you might want to start noting any of these wastes that exist in you culture, because you likely need to identify behaviors to counteract them.

When determining our new culture, we cannot forget the primary motivation in humans for

change: money, power, and status. This implies that you need to link your Cultural Transformation Plan to succession planning and personal development. If developing leadership abilities and identifying successors is not part of your plan, you will see both company and personal stagnation, which can send your star team members out in search of greener pastures. This link will be encouraged as you build you plan; it also becomes part of the coaching responsibility in Chapter 9. You also want to consider whether anxiety over the next promotion or bonus causes team members to hesitate or fall in line with the mob mentality when making decisions, and either one is contrary to the culture you desire.

Determining the Desired Mindset

A mindset identifies your mental world, outlines your personal objectives, and determines your professional objectives, and your new culture should determine a desired type of mindset.

Your mindset develops over many years and is heavily influenced in your early years by parents and teachers. It determines whether you are open to learning, or you know it all. Everyone has both open and closed mindsets:

- An open mindset allows growth and learning, assuming you can always do better.

- A closed mindset assumes someone's natural talents and abilities are responsible for determining success.

One trait desired for your new culture should be an open mindset, which creates a learning organization in which everyone can keep improving (that is, continuous improvement). It drives the courage and humility we will be discussing in Chapter 9, allowing acceptance of constructive criticism to guide you toward personal and organizational improvement. The more a closed mindset slips in, the more people sit back and wait for their natural talents to take over and make decisions, and they want to be right and are not interested in feedback to the contrary. This closed mindset can lead to the *CEO syndrome* (the organization operating according to the personality of either the CEO or founder, not according to the organization's mission/objectives; this results in only receiving filtered information that agrees with the CEO's views). If feeding the CEO's ego is a part of the current culture, obviously you have a considerable issue that should not be part of your new culture, you must consider the feasibility of rectifying this behavior, since it flies in the face of what you have defined as a desired culture. If the culture centers on rewarding people's inherent talents instead of their learning, there can be great difficulty in accepting news that something has not gone as planned and their image may be threatened. This can result in the extreme cases where mistakes are not admitted to investors, lies begin, and you might go down the road of Enron and others who have met similar fates.

Defining the Desired Culture for the Organization

Once you have done your best to analyze your existing culture at the organizational or plant level and come to terms with the reasons behind its development, you are ready to consider what traits are desired in your new culture (the future state for the organization). This new culture must support attaining your strategic objectives; therefore, the sequence suggested in this book is critical. If you consider you are ready to begin work on a Cultural Transformation Plan and have not yet worked through a cycle of strategic deployment as described in Chapter 3, I suggest you focus first on getting this right.

Assuming you are diligently working to evolve a strategy deployment process, and your current objectives are clear, well communicated, and supported by the various levels—and you have begun analyzing your current organizational culture to the best of your ability, you are ready to define the traits and beliefs you require in the new culture. The first question to ask is, are the current traits and beliefs (this should include values, norms, ideologies) acceptable and supporting of your strategic objectives? Rarely are all traits, behaviors and habits the desired ones, so we proceed assuming you require some improvements.

As mentioned in Chapter 1, a lean culture systematically develops people's qualities to include:

- Internal discipline

- Open to exposing problems

- Continuously improving processes

- Acceptance of change

- Willing to experiment to achieve a shared vision

- Small but continuous improvements

- Innovative and adaptive

- Continuously challenging

- Effective communication

- Have courage, humility and empathy

- An open mindset

- Opposition to Goldsmith's bad habits

- Proactive and conscientious

Parts of this list could become a starting point for your desired behaviors.

A second consideration when defining the desired culture is whether the team currently has the knowledge and structure to understand the external environment—and how that brings about the need for cultural and process changes. If you determine that key parts of your team do not possess the understanding of the external environment and its relationship to the necessary cultural changes, at this point you should be considering what qualities in the new culture could improve this. Naturally there will be actions outside the cultural aspects that will also support this, for example, new structures (i.e. flatter structure) within the business, and new types of communication (as discussed in the strategy deployment matrix).

An example of what everyone should understand about the external environment is that your competitors want you to conduct business the same way you have always been doing it. This makes you predictable and stagnate, allowing competitors a fantastic opportunity to plan strategies to gather more market share. On the other hand, if you are always changing methods and products/services, your unpredictableness is something the competition can't plan on.

As you are identifying the necessity for new traits and values, a third consideration must be whether top leadership can personally support these traits. Will they be able to act accordingly and reinforce these by teaching them to others? If you feel this is too much in conflict with the CEO's traits, it is unlikely a Cultural Transformation Plan will take root. In Chapter 7, I discuss a report that shows empirical data connecting a CEO's characteristics to the organizational culture. There is a high correlation in the areas of agreeableness and neuroticism (emotional instability), so if you believe that some of the new traits and behaviors you are targeting are against the CEO's beliefs, you need to review and possibly revise them.

As part of the change process, you need your CEO to influence the new characteristics by teaching, communicating (through stories), and symbolizing these new behaviors; if this is not in his or her blood, you are likely wasting your time.

As you consider the traits and behaviors required to reach your strategic objectives, it is worthwhile to discuss a few of Edgar Schein's five guidelines for a leader when changing an organizational culture. To begin with, "Don't assume the leader can manipulate culture."[12] Although leaders are used to controlling other aspects of the organization, culture is largely determined and controlled by the people within the company. Schein points out that the culture may end up controlling the leader. Another of his guidelines is, "Don't assume there is a correct culture, or that a strong culture is better than a weak one." The culture change should be viewed by the organization as a learning experience, and any good learning organization knows they will go through the PDCA loop in all cases. It is also logical that, as your strategic objectives and your environment changes, the culture will need to change with it. Finally, "don't assume all aspects of the organization's culture are important." There are certain elements, especially within the culture and subculture, which will have little impact on reaching your strategic objectives. It is leadership's responsibility to try to determine which of those characteristics are not critical to reaching your strategic objectives.

Defining a new culture will likely lead to identifying many items that need to change, in addition to the people's mentality. Some of these are systematic and physical, but they must be considered in your plan, as they have a consequence on the organization's mentality. These can include items like:

- Organizational structure (flat structures, redefined responsibilities, value stream management)

- Procedures (direct and transactional procedures revised)

- Work station layouts (create teamwork, create flow)

- Departmental and other physical layouts (open offices, no reserved parking)

- Executive perks and dress code

Objectives Written into the Cultural Transformation Plan

Now is the time to propose your desired soft objectives (or behavioral objectives). The recommended format is on Post-it Notes, although since photos do not clearly show the important details, you can view this as an Excel image (in the right-hand column of Figure 6.1, denoted at Step 1). First try summarizing (with bullet points) your most prevalent behavioral intentions. Behavioral issues involve creating awareness through training and using certain lean methodologies to reinforce these mentality changes, for example:

- A3 Problem Solving

- Visuals and five-minute stand-up meetings

- Empathy through better listening

- Extroversion increased by lunches with your team

- Coaching and training

- Conflict-management workshops

- Shifting-paradigms workshops

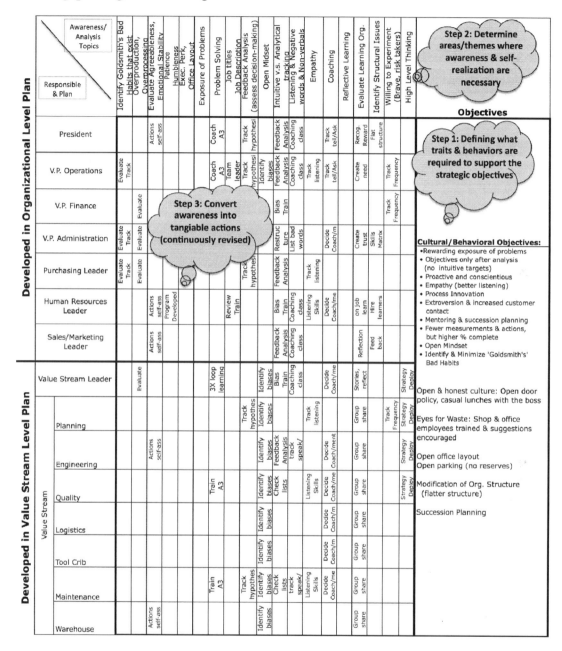

Figure 6.1 Cultural Transformation Plan

Implementing your plans with tangible actions could include regular PDCA of strategy deployment, putting in place new structures or new workstation layouts, requiring more analytical thinking, and so on. Later on, these awareness steps and tangible actions will be introduced into the body of the Cultural Transformation Plan.

The second section of the objectives box (in the lower half of the right hand column of Figure 6.1) contains more tangible and/or structural objectives that are identified as requirements to support the new culture. Examples of these would be an open-door policy, lunches with the leaders, open office layout, no reserved parking, and succession planning.

The format you use for your Cultural Transformation Plan is less significant than with the strategy deployment matrix (where the matrix guides you into questioning each department's interdependence with each objective). Regarding the proposed formats in this book, *don't adopt them, adapt them.* What is vital, though, is to have a clearly communicated and documented plan, because this demonstrates respect and removes the insecurity that comes with unclear expectations. Also for revising and follow-up, you want to commit this to paper. The remaining information shown in Figure 6.1 (Steps 2 and 3) is the focus of the remaining chapters in this book.

Defining the Desired Culture for Departments

As previously mentioned, some organizations struggle to analyze their current culture and the desired traits at an organizational or plant level. It is strongly recommended that you begin there, but if you struggle too much, the next step is to perform this at the value stream and departmental levels (or sometimes personal or positional levels when only one person fulfills a particular role). Engaging all leaders in defining the desired and current behaviors at the departmental or personal level is where the true awareness and buy-in take place and is key to the success of this technique. You will notice at this step it's actually better to first define the desired traits and behaviors (the future state) and then create awareness (the current state).

This refinement allows the individuals in those positions/departments to self-assess their own traits and compare to the desired ones. At the individual level you are really first defining the future state (desired behaviors) and then allowing each person over time to come to terms with his or her existing traits, which identifies the current state.

A practical way to begin facilitating this discussion, linking it to the strategy and gaining buy-in from those involved, is for each value stream to construct the matrix show in Figure 6.2A. Bringing together the leaders and functional representatives you can begin creating the headings for the rows based on the objectives in your annual strategy. The columns then become the functions that constitute the value stream, and you begin brainstorming the predominant soft skills (behaviors and traits), which are required to meet or exceed the objectives. Figure 6.2A shows a team working through developing this matrix, Figure 6.2B shows this matrix reformatted making it easier to read.

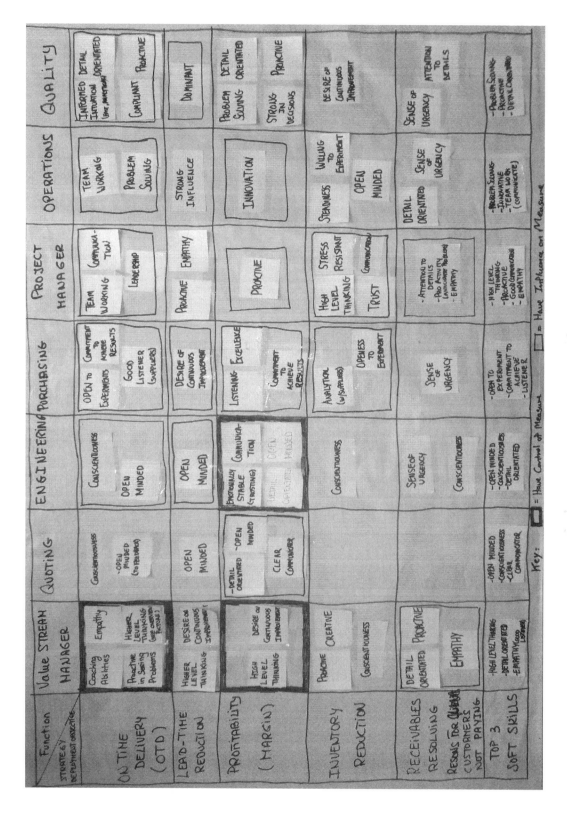

Figure 6.2 A Practical Matrix to Guide the Team in Aligning Desired Departmental Traits with the Strategy

FUNCTION / Strategy Deployment Objective	Value Stream Manager	Quoting	Engineering	Purchasing	Project Manager	Operations	Quality
On Time Delivery (OTD)	-Coaching abilities -Empathy -Proactive in seeing problems -Higher level thinking (see overview picture)	-Conscientiousness -Open Minded (to feedback)	-Conscientiousness -Open Minded	-Open to experiments -Commitment to achieve results -Good listener (suppliers)	-Team working -Communication -Leadership	-Team working -Problem solving	-Informed intuation (fast, analytical) -Detail Orientated -Compliant -Proactive
Lead-Time Reduction	-Higher level thinking -Desire of Continuous Improvement	-Open Minded	-Open Minded	-Desire of Continuous Improvement	-Proactive -Empathy	-Strong Influence	-Dominant
Profitability (Margin)	-High level thinking -Desire on Continuous Improvement	-Detail Orientated -Open Minded -Clear communicator	-Emotionally Stable (trusting) -Detail Orientated -Open Minded -Communication	-Listening -Excellence -Commitment to achieve results	-Proactive	-Innovation	-Problem solving -Detail Orientated -Strong in decisions -Proactive
Inventory Reduction	-Proactive -Creative -Conscientiousness		-Conscientiousness	-Analytical (w/ suppliers) -Openess to experiment	-High level thinking -stress resistant -trust -Communication	-Steadiness -Willing to Experiment -Open Minded	-Desire for Continuous Improvement
Receivables - resolving reasons for customers not paying	- Detail Orientated - Proactive - Empathy		- Sense of urgency - Conscientiousness	-Sense of urgency	-Attention to Details - Pro activity (anticipate problems) - Empathy	-Detail Orientated -Sense of urgency	- Sense of urgency - Attention to Details
Top 3 soft skills	- High level thinking - Detail Orientated - Empathy (good listener)	-Open Minded -Conscientiousness -Clear communicator	-Open Minded -Conscientiousness -Detail Orientated	-Open to Experiment -Commitment to achieve -Listener	- High level thinking -Proactive -Good Communication - Empathy	-Problem Solving -Innovative -Team Work (communicate)	-Problem Solving -Proactive -Detail Orientated

Have **Control** of measure

Have **Influence** on measure

Figure 6.2B A Practical Matrix to Guide the Team in Aligning Desired Departmental Traits with the Strategy

In this company the team also considered where those traits had either the most control or influence in reaching the targets, helping better define the top 3 desired traits for each position/department (shown in the bottom row of Figure 6.2B). This matrix is usually built on either a white-board or with Post-its. You should use this method to lead catch-ball with your team, it not only creates buy-in but begins developing self-awareness. This matrix is the first step for identifying the actions in the value stream portion (bottom of matrix) of the Cultural Transformation Plan (shown in Figure 6.1). You might decide there is no need to display then entire plan (both top leadership and value stream levels) within one visual as shown in Figure 6.1, and naturally that's fine, remember not to adopt it, but adapt it.

Summary

I recommend going through this process (defining the necessary traits and behaviors) after having clearly communicated strategic objectives and completing an in-depth analysis of your current culture.

Some of the ways recommended to analyze the existing culture are:

- Utilizing the list of "Concepts Defining an Organization's Culture" at the beginning of this chapter, define how these manifest themselves in your company.

- Observe how problems are recognized and resolved.

- What type of words do the leaders use to encourage teamwork and ownership of problems?

- Identify all existing cultures and subcultures.

- Review M. Goldsmith's 20 bad habits and determine whether some of them exist in your organization.

- Observe whether people try to keep busy resulting in over-production and over-processing.

- How are annual objectives communicated and deployed?

The recommended ways to define your desired culture:

- Define traits and behaviors necessary to support strategic objectives.

- Determine whether the team has the knowledge and structure to understand the needs of the external environment.

- Review Edgar Shein's five guidelines of when a leader changes the organizational culture.

- Engage the value stream by building the matrix show in Figure 6.2

The next step (in Chapter 7) is to individually analyze your leadership team's current traits and behaviors so those can be assessed against your newly defined behavioral needs. Some organizations are concerned that by first establishing your desired traits and behaviors (assuming these are shared with the leadership team) they will taint the self-assessments that will be introduced in the next chapter. The idea of people aligning their responses toward what they perceived are the desired answers is a possibility to consider (though some of the assessment tools have control items embedded to minimize this). My experience has been that this is the best sequence and that the advantages outweigh the disadvantages, although naturally this is your choice. Figure 6.3 shows the recommend steps to this point.

Steps to Mental Transformation Plan

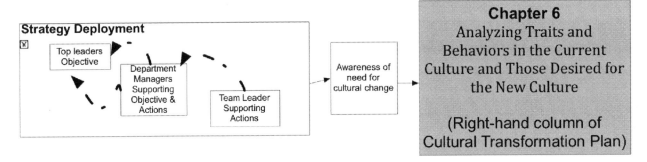

Figure 6.3 Process Steps through Chapter 6

CHAPTER 7

Analysis for the Cultural Transformation Plan

Your organization's cultural is a management tool that helps create a competitive advantage. Cultural change begins with strategy deployment, followed by understanding the organization's current culture and then determining the desired traits and behaviors for each position or department to support all of the strategic objectives. The most successful way to open someone's mind to change is involving them and creating self-awareness, therefore the next step is to work as a team and brainstorm the best possible ways to gain an individual self-awareness for each of the desired traits. Finally the team should share thoughts on what actions can help to change specific behaviors.

Creating Awareness and Identifying Actions to Achieve the Desired Traits

Following on from the value stream team creating the desired traits to support the strategic objectives (shown in Figure 6.2), the next steps involve: 1) How you can create awareness for each desired trait identified and 2) What possible actions the team member could consider if he/she is becomes aware their current traits are not aligned with the desired traits.

The best way I have found for a team to work through this is gathering the value stream leader and their team, based on the matrix developed in Figure 6.2, brainstorm how you can create awareness for each of the desired traits previously identified. Although this is often done on a white board or with post-its, this is more legibly displayed by the recreation shown in Figure 7.1. In this figure you see one box taken from the previous matrix and for each desired trait, possibilities of how to create awareness are listed. You can see this requires effort, though each department is only responsible for their column of the desired traits that were identified in Figure 6.2.

After creating awareness of the person's existing abilities, the team can also brainstorm what possible actions could be undertaken to alter the behavior or habits (displayed in the lower right-hand corner of 7.1).

Creating Awareness (ideas of what can be tracked or undertaken for assessing your current state)

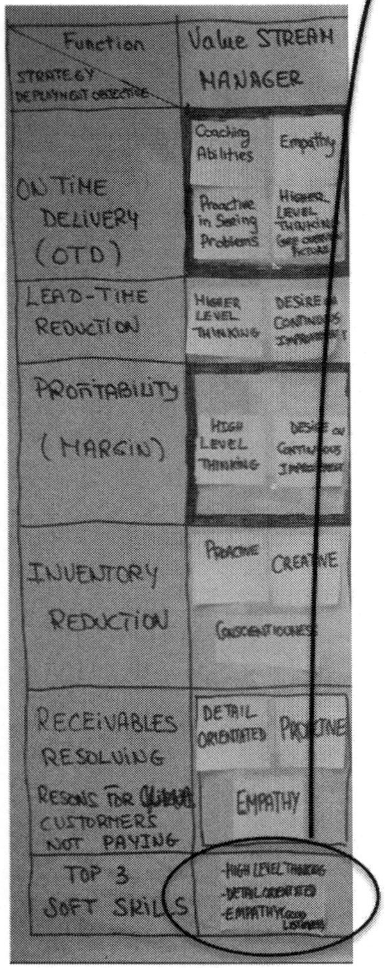

Higher Level Thinking
- How often have you moved/loaned valuable members outside your division for the overall benefit of the company?
- How often have you suggested ideas to be implemented outside your value stream level?
- How many have been acted upon? Quantity of your team for which you have helped evolve a Personal Development Plan?
- How often do you visit other companies to learn and improve?
- Do you support projects in other value streams?
- What proportion of your time is spent on long term planning and follow-up? (i.e. next quarter, next year, next three years?)
- Do you actively participate in the development of the medium term strategy?

Detail Orientated
- Take Goldberg's 'Big Five Personality Inventory' Assessment paying attention to how you score on *conscientiousness*.
- How often do you experience a problem that you notice you should have been anticipated?
- How often are you coaching your members to realize an issue they did not notice?
- How often do you root cause problem solve after the first occurrence?
- How often do you anticipate problems versus reacting & firefighting problems

Empathy
- Take DISC (Discovery) Assessment (to determine behavior in various situations).
- Monitor (for some period) you ratio of time spent listening versus speaking.
- How often do you act based on input from team members (instead of an isolated decision)?
- Take Goldberg's 'Big Five Personality Inventory' Assessment paying attention to how you score on emotional instability.
- How often do you present negative body language (i.e. distracted, looking angry, no eye contact) ?
- Should be assessed by an associate.
- How often are you focused on the health, safety and well-being of your team?

Possible Actions to Change Behavior

Higher Level Thinking
- Business classes (MBA type) and financial type training.
- Lead improvements for direct & indirect processes (i.e. Value Stream Mapping & Process Mapping)
- Lead strategy deployment reviews, revisions and follow-up.
- Recognize your biases and work to minimize their influence.

Detail Orientated
- No setting objectives without involvement (i.e. no 'stretch' targets without engagement from team).
- Coach people using A3 in problem solving and developing strategies.
- Increase time spent reviewing and on GEMBA walks.
- Utilizing action lists for follow-up and coaching.

Empathy
- Monitor & improve time spent listening vs. time spent speaking
- More head nods and rephrasing when others are speaking to you.
- Increase socialization (i.e. team lunches).
- Work to become more extroverted (i.e. speaking in front of groups, starting conversations with strangers).
- Focus to improve body language & use affirmative actions of comprehension when listening (i.e. paraphrase, head nods).

For the desired traits, identify how to create self awareness of the individuals current state

For each desired trait, identify actions to help change the behavior

Figure 7.1 Creating Awareness and Identifying Actions to Achieve the Desired Traits

Personal Awareness Created through Self-Assessments

You will note in Figure 7.1 that the team had some prior knowledge of personality self-assessments thereby allowing them to link the appropriate assessment with the desired trait for which it could help in creating non-biased awareness. I find many companies associate and utilize some of these personality assessments as a screening tool in the hiring process (becoming so predominate that in 2011 the Equal Employment Opportunity Commission had to become involved in ruling them as an acceptable part of a company's screening process), but most do not consider the value in utilizing the assessments for creating awareness of behaviors with the existing team members. Now we will explore some of the recommended personality assessments and how they can be used in creating awareness.

By first determining the desired traits for your cultural transformation, you may taint the results of the self-assessment tools that are suggested in this chapter. By establishing what you desire in the new, lean culture, you might guide some of the team toward skewing the self-assessments (discussed in this chapter) if they are not answered honestly, and this is more likely to happen if people believe they recognize the preferred answers. Although experience has shown that the sequence I've recommended is the best one, this downside can be mitigated by encouraging honesty in answering these voluntary self-assessments, as this is part of a leader's personal development. Also some assessments contain control questions to try and identify inconsistencies.

The comparison between our current traits and our desired traits can be brutal, so be careful when handling and sharing the results. Remember that the results likely imply that leadership's existing traits and behaviors can use some realignment, and that is not comfortable information at most organizations. It is critical, too, that leadership not utilize assessments in a bureaucratic fashion to demand results; instead, they should first let individuals review them and decide whether they are valid and worthwhile to share with the team.

The underlying assumptions at this point are that top leadership desires a change to reach certain objectives and recognizes some of the bad habits in the current culture. They have begun the first step of an enterprise-wide strategy deployment, although they still might not understand all that is implied by this change or the intense effort necessary for cultural change. But the desire to make a change should exist when reaching this step, knowing the reward will offset the work in getting there.

You must also take into account that not every manager can transform into a leader; there may be certain inherit traits, behaviors, or bad habits that managers are unwilling or unable to change. Therefore, part of the process is to identify anyone who will not be able to develop to the desired level in the new culture and decide accordingly what should be done within the structure. Remember that a successful organization does not require everyone to be a leader; you can reach an improved status with some managers among your ranks.

This chapter suggests some impartial methods to help in determining what you are good at through self-assessments. Although this will have implications outside your working life, we focus the discussion on how this information can be used in personal development that benefits the desired organizational culture. We focus on discovering and building from your strengths, as this is usually more productive and successful than "changing what you are not good at," but it's also worthwhile for you to consider where you might impact your weaknesses in a successful manner. Taking the pragmatic approach, it is easier to stop certain behaviors (with others helping identify when they occur) than to adapt new and unfamiliar ones; therefore, your priority will be first stopping bad habits, and then adopting new behaviors.

The suggestions in this chapter both create awareness and analyze where you should focus your cultural transformation. Most people think they know what they are and are not good at, but the situation is usually more complex than that.

I discovered some of these tools years ago when deciding to jump out of corporate America and look toward operating my own business. Determined to buy a small company instead of creating something from the ground up, I discovered that almost more important than the due-diligence in evaluating companies (such as profit-and-loss analysis and financial-and-market projections) was to evaluate my own strengths and weakness that I would be bringing to the company. Although I was confident in my effectiveness and where my behavior excelled in specific situations, some honest friends and family had slightly different opinions. This led me to looking for quick, easy, and non-biased ways to determine my strengths and weaknesses in decision-making and in my work life, to ensure where I would have the most positive effects to leverage the success of my venture. Some of the following tools resulted from that search.

Key Areas for Creating Awareness

To start establishing the current status of a company's ability to accept change, I will share my experience and understanding in a few key areas:

- Personal effectiveness and behavioral assessments

- Intuitive versus analytical thoughts in decision-making

- Leading without power (leadership improved through coaching)

- Creating a learning environment (or learning organization)

These crucial steps toward building your Cultural Transformation Plan will be discussed over the next few chapters. I am providing a pragmatic way to move forward by first defining which traits and behaviors are desired, and then assessing at a personal level which norms currently exist (organizations typically have a diverse group of personalities that cover most aspects), in order to facilitate the development of a transformational plan.

Cultural acceptance is the key to having a successful lean conversion; awareness and analysis are the first steps. Behavioral change can never be forced; if there is going to be a chance of success, it must first come from awareness and creating a desire for change. The internal discipline required for this journey is often beyond the current quick fix or *immediate-results culture* you might have, but after reading this book you will have an outline of some practical and proven techniques to increase awareness and your chances of success.

CEO Characteristics versus Organizational Culture

Founders and top leaders entrench their personality into organizations through the objectives they set. This typically attracts people with similar characteristics and values, thereby strongly influencing the organizational culture. Therefore, prior to looking at the other soft cultural steps, you need to understand how important the CEO's influence is in transforming a culture, and what proven relationships exist between top leadership traits and the organization's culture. There is the obvious importance of what the boss pays attention to, what key performance indicators he or she values and how rewards are allocated, but on the soft side, CEOs also look for a balance between people like themselves and those who make up for their shortcomings, to help in achieving company's goals.

You might recall in the previous chapter it was mentioned that we should not assume a CEO can manipulate culture, and it is largely determined and controlled by the work force. Although this is true, there are two areas in which the CEO's traits link precisely to the organizational culture: agreeableness and neuroticism (two of the five categories in Goldberg's Big Five Personality Inventory).[13] These have an effect on the team's behavior, interaction, and, most importantly, team decision-making. (This study involved CEOs from small- to mid-sized organizations.)

Agreeableness here means being compassionate, considerate, friendly, generous, and helpful. *Neuroticism* (also know as *emotional instability*) is the propensity to experience negative emotions, meaning they are more likely than the average to experience feelings like anxiety, anger, envy, guilt, and depression.

It is critical to understand where your top leadership scores on agreeableness and neuroticism, as they have this high correlation in influencing the culture. There is no way to tone down the importance of beginning your self-assessments with your top leaders and quickly comparing the results to the desired traits and behaviors that support meeting your strategic objectives. If top leadership scores low on agreeableness, they are usually not considerate, not friendly, and not very helpful. This is not entirely bad, as you will want a balanced leadership team, with some scoring in the medium range who will challenge decisions and introduce a critical eye. Very low scorers tend to see people as being dishonest and do not naturally trust them; obviously, this is not in line with a lean culture and deserves attention.

High neuroticism scorers have a tendency to respond poorly to environmental stress, often view ordinary situations as threatening, and they may have trouble controlling urges and delaying gratification. These are also traits not in line with a lean culture or where your organization desires to go. Ideally, your CEO will score medium to high on agreeableness and low on neuroticism (emotional instability).

The point is, if your top leadership does *not* appear to have the correct orientation of agreeableness and emotional instability, it is unlikely the organization's culture can overcome them. In other areas of the leadership's personality, for example, openness, conscientiousness, extraversion (per Goldberg's Big Five Personality Traits), there are lower correlations between the culture and top leadership's personality traits; therefore, if your CEO is not in line with the objectives in these areas, the organization's culture might be able to overcome them. So if you decide to follow the recommendation of utilizing some of these self-assessments, the check point is to have the top leaders complete Goldberg's Big Five Personality Inventory, and if they score low in agreeableness category and/or high in neuroticism, you will likely need to evaluate your options before making a Cultural Transformation Plan with the remaining leaders.

Ideally, you can come to terms with the alignment between the desired organizational cultural traits and how the CEO's characteristics might limit a successful transformation. These are difficult issues to even talk about in an organizational hierarchy, but if there is serious desire from the top, there should be serious consideration given to what has been empirically proven. This study (and its footnoted data) may be worth sharing, as the data from this study can remove some of the emotion and allow others to approach this more analytically.

Utilizing Behavior and Personal-Effectiveness Assessments

Obviously, I am not a psychologist and understand only in layman's terms a bit of psychology as applied to personality traits and preferences in decision-making. That said, I am going to recommend some self-assessments from practitioners and psychologists that I find useful at this step in the journey. To help in assessing the organization's willingness to change, you need to first analyze the leadership's current mental state and develop a plan to overcome resistance. A lot of this must come through self-recognition (in this case, self-assessment). There are many off-the-shelf questionnaires that help in determining personality preferences, although many are inadequate and of those that can be helpful, it will be your responsibility to determine the appropriateness of the following suggestions.

The easiest way to proceed is for you to first personally complete these assessments, and then review how valuable they are in increasing awareness and determining a personal Cultural Transformation Plan. Then, as previously discussed, you might want your CEO to at least complete Goldberg's Big Five Personality Inventory to ensure there are not any concerns with his or her outcomes in the categories of agreeableness or neuroticism/emotional instability.

You can take these assessments to an extreme, but I suggest only the few that I have found most appropriate to cover the dimensions necessary. They are all quick and easy—best of all, they are free of charge. The interpretation is generally easy, but centers on your effort and inclination; it will become whatever you decide to make of it. I am recommending three and a possible a fourth in the sections that follow, although there are many available and you're encouraged to do your own research. There are few independent studies published, and various criticisms can be found, although I leave you to be the judge, as these are the best personality and decision-making assessments currently available. I also provide a list of a few others that are available, although some of these have a cost associated with them.

Note: Online pre-employment tests, which are actually personality assessments based on large data sets, have become so popular that in 2011 the EEOC (Equal Employment Opportunity Commission) began drafting plans to enforce how they are used.[14] The concerns are not with the assessments themselves, but with the manner in which the results are being utilized. For pre-employment, the purpose is to evaluate traits as the basis for the hiring decision, but this results in one-directional assessment without any feedback, causing the tests to periodically come under fire from those who did not get the job—they question whether a bias was involved. As long as the questions are relevant to the work, they have been ruled as legal and help employers select better candidates. In the methodology to follow, we are at the other extreme in both purpose and the level of participation when suggesting to utilize personality assessments. You will discover a much more positive experience based on:

- The individual has the option whether or not to participate after clearly understanding that this is to help with personal development and certain organizational objectives.

- The results are to be privately viewed with the opportunity to share the outcomes.

Keep in mind the purpose of these non-biased self-assessments is to create awareness at individual level of personalities (traits and behaviors) as they apply to decision-making. Although you may feel you know the team and understand their beliefs and traits, only self-discovery opens the possible motivation for change. Remember, we often wrongly assess our personalities and those of others.

Big Five Personality Inventory (Goldberg): The Link Between Personality and Behavior

Contemporary psychology recognizes five broad dimensions of personality often referred to as the Big Five personality factors (Costa and McCrae, 1992). They helps us in recognizing the link between someone's personality and various behaviors. The big five factors are: openness, conscientiousness, extraversion, agreeableness, and neuroticism/emotional instability.

The traits corresponding to the big five are:

- **Openness to experience:** Could be expressed as a creative and curious person instead of someone steady and careful. He or she would be more emotional, adventurous with ideas, and seeking different experiences. For most cultural transformation, you would want a mix of high and medium scores in this area.

- **Conscientiousness:** Is someone organized and efficient, not sloppy or laid-back. They would be characterized as having self-discipline, being achievers, and planning most things. For your cultural transformation, you would want a majority of leadership with a high score in this category.

- **Extraversion:** As implied, this person is outgoing and has lots of energy, instead of being introverted and reserved. They are usually positive and like to socialize. Regarding this trait, you'll likely target a mix of high and medium scores in your team; too many strong extroverts are undesirable.

- **Agreeableness:** Someone who is friendly, compassionate, cooperative instead of being cold and standoffish. They trust mankind and are not suspicious or antagonistic. This is a trait where you generally target high scores, although a minority with low scores will introduce criticalness and cause you to thoroughly justify your decisions.

- **Neuroticism (often referred to as emotional instability):** Someone with a strong likelihood to experience negative emotions like anxiety, anger, guilt, and depression. You would tend to become angry or depressed quite easily. You would target low scores here, desiring the opposite, a person who is more positive, calm, and relaxed.

The self-assessment of these five factors is a good baseline to use because it is comprehensive and data driven. After completing Goldberg's 45 questions, you receive a ranking in percentile for each category, showing how you score against others who have participated. To get started, you can go to www.outofservice.com/bigfive (or other websites offering the assessment), complete the assessment in a few minutes, and immediately receive your results (for free).

Remember that you are trying to objectively establish the current status of your team's personality, traits, and behaviors in comparison to the future requirements of the organization. Answering the questions honestly is key to receiving useful feedback. Sometimes the answers are not what you expect or want to hear, and you will have to consider the implications of the results as they reveal weak spots.

The advantage of the self-assessment is that your personality is scored in comparison to others who have taken the personality assessment. The percentage you receive for each of the five factors is relative to the others who have taken this online test (the only downside is you do not know how large the total sample size is). The percentile indicates the percentage of people who have scored less on each factor; the higher your score the more of that trait you have. For example, if you score a high percentile on "openness to experience," you are more original, creative, and curious. If your strategic objectives and your cultural objectives require more creativity, you are in luck; if not, consider what would make you more creative.

Print your results and compare them to the desired cultural objectives you previously identified in Chapter 6. Now decide how publically you want to share out, keeping in mind that if you want a balanced team, you need to also compare the working group's outcomes. Each team member will have a different level of comfort in sharing these results; the best situation is for your top leadership to complete the assessments first and to be open with their results. That will likely pave the way for public sharing among all team members.

Assuming top leadership completed the self-assessment, evaluate their results, specifically for "agreeableness" and "neuroticism" against any related desired culture traits. If the top leader's score is in opposition to your cultural objectives (usually you are targeting high percentiles in agreeableness and low percentiles in neuroticism), it is a good time to stop and reflect, especially if you do not have general agreement that you can overcome this. Is there a feeling that actions can be identified and a level of confidence that the end justifies the means? If not you must stop and consider the value in going further with analysis for a Cultural Transformation Plan. This applies only to top leadership's personality in the areas of agreeableness and neuroticism; studies have not found a strong correlation with the CEO's scores in openness, conscientiousness, and extraversion in effecting a cultural change. In other words, in these additional three areas, the CEO has less influence and the team can likely direct and move the culture, independent of the CEO's personality traits.

DISC Assessment: Behavior in Environments and Situations

Based on the work of Dr. William Marston, the DISC assessment is unique in that it examines the behavior and preferences of individuals in their environment within a specific situation. You can take the DISC assessment free of charge online at various websites, for example, www.123test.com/disc-personality-test/.

It groups the individual into four behavioral styles: dominance, influence, steadiness and compliance (thereby creating the acronym DISC). Although we all posses a portion of each of these styles, the assessment distributes (based on a total 100 percent) a percentage to each category. There are not clear distinctions from one behavior to the next, and they blend together differently. By understanding our primary behavior, secondary behavior, and the rest, we can use the results to better understand:

- How we can function in a team and the composition of our teams

- The corresponding traits and behaviors associated with either a high or low score in a particular category; you can assess these against those traits you are trying to move toward in the new culture

There are 25 groups with four statements each contained in the assessment tool; you select the statement considered most representative of yourself and also select the one you consider least like you. It takes only 10 to 15 minutes, and you can click to receive the test results immediately. You will need to determine whether the test report will be privately viewed or shared within the leadership team. The results show the various percentages distributed within the four categories, and it is immediately obvious which are your first and second areas of dominance.

The most useful section of the test report is the description of the traits related to the four categories; these help you to better understand your strengths and weaknesses. It is interesting to compare the traits and behaviors where you scored high with those that the organization desires. If you scored low on an area that is considered critical for the new culture, you should consider noting that in the Cultural Transformation Plan and determining what actions are appropriate. But keep in mind that changing human characteristics and mental traits is not an easy road—but that road does start with awareness.

Some criticize assessments that require stating preferences between various terms, as opposed to those that require you to answer or scale a statement. That said, it is difficult to find hard data on the accuracy of the DISC test. Although this is an older assessment, more recent correlation coefficients have demonstrated that it holds a reasonable connection. The DISC has also recently been refined by psychologists and HR experts, and the newer version is called the Discovery Personality Test, which you can research and decide the applicability of this newer variant. So first take the test on your own and then, after reviewing and evaluating your results, decide whether another colleague or two should also complete it to determine the assessment's applicability to the wider leadership team. With all these evaluations, ensure this is done on a voluntary basis, and also allow the participants to view their results privately before deciding whether to share with the team.

The ROPELOC: Review of Personal Effectiveness

This tool is different and complements the DISC assessment by looking more at personal effectiveness in life. It has a wide-ranging audience having been successfully used with executives as well as high school students. Developed by Garry E. Richards, Louise Ellis, and James T. Neill in 2000, it is a newer test that has been refined over a number of years and has been utilized by a large number of participants. There is also more data to show distinct correlations with the tool's results. The tool also includes control items to allow a baseline comparison for changes. Personal effectiveness (the assessment's objective) can be defined as a person's ability to survive and successfully adapt. It can help determine areas of personal development that imply more specifically where one can focus to improve if so desired. This is also free to complete although the analysis can be performed in a variety of ways.

The conditions for use are stated on the following website: http://wilderdom.com/tools/leq/ROPELOC.html. On this link, in the top right hand corner, you will see the various downloads available. If you download ROPELOC Insturment.doc, you will have the instructions and the 45 questions. This assessment takes about 10–15 minutes to complete, and the easiest way to view the results is to create a simple Excel spreadsheet based on your average combined answer for each of the 14 categories:

- Active involvement
- Cooperative teamwork
- Leadership ability
- Open thinking
- Quality seeking
- Self confidence
- Self efficacy

- Social effectiveness
- Stress management
- Time efficiency
- Coping with change
- Overall effectiveness
- Internal locus of control
- External locus of control

There are also 2 answers utilized as control items. The ROPELOC factors and their corresponding descriptions can also be downloaded on the website I mentioned, it is also in the top right-hand corner of the website, it is the ROPELOC Factors.doc . Each of the ROPELOC factors are associated with three of the questions, and I usually take an average of the three questions for each category and plot that in a bar chart. I have also included a simple Excel spreadsheet I created to view the results; it is displayed in Appendix E and can easily be reproduced in Excel. If you would like a copy of the Excel file, please send an email request to: ropeloc@strategic-leaders.com.

You will note that, in the example in Appendix E, I have put John Smith's answers in for the 45 questions, then the spreadsheet groups and averages his answers for the 14 ROPELOC factors, you can see this in the formulas shown and then it is displayed in the bar chart. In this example John answered many of the questions high on the scale of "true, like me." You will note that most of the ROPELOC factors are positive behaviors or traits and many of these would be desirable for your new culture. In this case, John Smith might be an ideal leader in your organization. Remember: it is important to determine which of these ROPELOC factors are most important for your new culture, or you will end up trying for the ideal situation in all 14 categories.

With this test, you end up with a score showing a self-assessment of how you see yourself on the 14 factors. Depending on the level of comfort with this data, you can look at each factor across the team and focus on the ones you feel are most important (based on your desired behaviors). This has a natural link for each member of the leadership team in designing his or her own Cultural Transformation Plan. So this is a tool that is better than most, and key to tapping into the psychological and behavioral aspects of human effectiveness in a variety of areas. This is also an interesting tool to use after transforming your culture for a period of time and seeing how various leaders' answers are affected or change.

Myers-Briggs Type Indicator: Assessing a Team for a Balance of Traits and Behaviors

Another worthwhile assessment tool, although the analysis is short and requires a little interpretation, is the Myers-Briggs Type Indicator. Again it has a different focus, it examines how people perceive the world and make decisions. I think it is important to complete in addition to the other assessments because the focus is on the person's preferences, which affect their decision-making. Since we need teams made of people who see the world differently (or have different attitudes), you should complete this and see if your team has some kind of balance. If your team's preferences are not balanced, this might also influence your Cultural Transformation Plan in terms of organizational structure. This works based on considering the rational (thinking and feeling) function and the irrational (sensing and intuition) function; it assumes that people are either born with or develop preferred ways of thinking and acting.

The Myers-Briggs assessment is also fast and simple, you can take it online by answering 72 questions in a yes or no format. The test can be found at www.humanmetrics.com/cgi-win/jtypes2.asp and plenty of other websites.

The results you receive are grouped you into four pairs of personality types; basically, each pair is contradictory. For example, extraversion versus introversion, sensing versus intuition, thinking versus feeling, and judgment versus perception. The results place you within one of 16 possible combinations of these attributes, using a four-letter acronym of your type and providing a short qualitative analysis showing whether you are slightly, moderately, or heavily expressed within the four attributes for your type.

One of the ways I find this assessment useful is to compare the types within the various leadership teams to see whether you have balance. Remember, there is not a right or wrong type, and the four preferences you have are exactly that . . . preferences. For example, if you are assessed with a J for judgment, it does not imply you are necessarily more judgmental or less perceptive, only that it is your preference. If your team is not balanced with preferences, it might be worthwhile to consider how important this is in your decision-making abilities and how it could be rectified—and perhaps also included in your Cultural Transformation Plan. Another way to use the results are to read the attributes associated with each of your preferences and see whether those are in line with the traits and behaviors you have defined as desirable for your new organizational culture. If not, decide whether this can be improved and whether to include it in your individual Cultural Transformation Plan.

Other Assessment Tools for Consideration

The following tools can also be considered as they offer different approaches and might expose some additional opportunities for your plan. I will very briefly mention a limited number of them, and you will have to decide if they deserve further research.

- **Personal Effectiveness Scale:** 15 questions are scaled from 0–4, depending how characteristic the statement is, as it applies toward you. Although the accuracy has been debated, the scoring categorizes you into 1 of 8 possible categories, although only the first category, "effective," would be considered positive, while the other seven are all negative. If you want to point out weaknesses, this tool can be useful, although I see it as a bit negative.

- **Johari Window:** This is more of a team exercise during which each member chooses five or six adjectives (form a list of 56) that he or she feels best describe the person's own personality.

Then colleagues of that person pick five or six adjectives they feel describe the same person. The adjectives are then mapped onto a four-quadrant grid (also called *the four rooms*). Room 1 is the part we and others see; room 2 includes the aspects others see but of which we are unaware; room 3 is where the subconscious part of us is neither seen by ourselves nor others; room 4 is a private space that we know of but we keep others out of. This is more of a tool to identify shortcomings in intellectual maturity. The objective is to show the open, hidden, blind spots and unknown areas that should provide a perspective into the individual's personality. For me, this one seems more personal than the others and a bit touchy-feely.

- **Herrmann Brian Dominance Instrument and Keirsey Temperament Sorter:** These are used to describe thinking preferences and a personality test for organizational and career development, respectively. These are more robust instruments and have a cost associated with them. They both have their place, although I suggest starting with the simple and free assessments first (and see the value they provide toward developing a Cultural Transformation Plan), before moving into these more elaborate and costly tools.

I have found it easiest to continue your awareness and start the analysis for your cultural change by first determining where you want to end up. Defining the desired culture in words and concepts is critical (this is shown in the right-hand column of the Cultural Transformation Plan, based on Chapter 6), although some find doing this first taints those self-assessing their personalities and they, in turn, might answer the assessments in a manner they feel will show they are ideal for the new culture (and, therefore, do not need to change anything in their mentality). Once you determine to either do this before or after completing individual assessments, it is time to determine which assessments are the best fit for your organization. I recommend three or four of the simple-and-easy tools: Big Five Personality Inventory, DISC, the ROPELOC, and the Myers-Briggs Type Indicator, because they focus on different areas and ensure that you have a wide focus for where you might need to concentrate your individually aligned Cultural Transformation Plan. There were also four other tools described that could be of help; consider these against organizational needs.

Intuitive versus analytical thinking is such a vital subject in a lean transformation that I have dedicated Chapter 8 to exploring this in some depth. The same applies to leading without power (which includes developing leadership through coaching skills); this also deserves a separate focus and is discussed in Chapter 9.

Possible Actions/Solutions for Personality Traits

The next step, after taking one or more of the assessments, is to settle on the implications of the results, in relation to achieving your objectives. Regarding what actions you may deem necessary and which should be incorporated into your plan, I will discuss this in two aspects. First, for actions considered important to improve personality traits, as most of the modern research demonstrates attainable results in this area, I will offer some options for what can be done toward improving decision-making abilities.

Some say recognizing the problem is half the battle, and that is the reason self-assessments are recommended. *Problem* might be a strong word in the case of our personality traits; *bad habits* is likely more acceptable. But whatever you call it, any difference between the current status and your desired traits is something we want to minimize. Psychologists and anthropologists agree that parts of our personalities can be altered, and many have found success following various four- or five-step improvement methodologies. If you break down the proven sequences from many of the psychologists, they are all similar to the steps I am suggesting in the Cultural Transformation Plan (except that most psychologists are focusing on changing personality traits more for personal reasons), they all look at some type of awareness (*why* change?), deciding *what* you want to change, giving yourself time to change in the right environment (*how* to change), following up, and using other people as support or utilizing rewards. This is similar to the sequence presented to this book, although we don't need to think of it as psychological: we have looked at the *why* (because our external environment is changing and we need to change to reach our breakthrough objectives), the *what* (what to change is determined through setting your objectives and assessing your current status against those objectives), and now we begin thinking of *how* to change.

Changes to personality traits are reflected by alterations in the brain; in other words, to modify your traits, you need to reconfigure your brain. Although it may sound impossible, it has been proven that changes can be made. Recently, lots of research has demonstrated that personality traits change more in adulthood than in childhood.[15] The personality traits (behaviors) you have today are a result of unique configurations in your brain. Modern psychologists have grouped these traits into five factors (as discussed in the Big Five Personality Inventory), and four of the five have been associated with distinct parts of the brain. This is based on the relationship between the volumes in that part of the brain versus the amount of that trait you possess. The only exception is "openness to experience," which cannot be related to any specific part of the brain and is more a result of the other four traits combined. Although we don't need to go any further into the left brain-right brain type discussions in this book, suffice it to say, there is a lot of new evidence that suggests that, with effort and exposure to the right environment, traits can change, and this happens more in adulthood than in childhood.

Your brain changes its wiring according to your behaviors, and because you can alter your behavior, your brain will accommodate. For example, if you begin entering situations where you are rewarded for socializing, you will become more extroverted and optimistic. So, that means you need to create an environment in the organization that encourages and rewards this. If you are placed in an environment where planning ahead and following thorough are shown to achieve your goals, you will change your behavior in this direction and become more conscientious. All that said, you must alter your behavior long enough to allow these regions of the brain to reconfigure themselves (to have new pathways form) and, unfortunately, this time period is not well defined. Although you know some of the lean methodologies and tools can help support this, I will provide more specifics on identifying: 1) the potential dangers of excessive intuitive thinking, 2) becoming a better coach, and 3) moving toward leadership in Chapters 8 through 10.

Now what can you do, practically speaking? Let's move through each of the Big Five Personality traits and talk about ideas to improve those behavior/traits, if you deem them necessary in achieving your objectives. The assumption is that you want to increase your score (your percentile in comparison to other assessment respondents), except in the case of neuroticism, which you want to decrease.

It is easier to stop a bad habit than adapt a new behavior or trait; therefore, minimizing any bad habits identified by the self-assessments should be the first priority, as you will have a higher likelihood of success. Following this, focus on the subsequent sequence to adapt new behaviors.

- Increasing your *openness to experience* is a result of improving the other traits, for example, being extroverted, more social, less afraid of new things, organized, and/or compassionate will help in creating more curiosity and openness to new ideas. This is critical for organizations that require innovation and creativity. Changing the structure to encourage more socialization, exposure of problems, questioning, and learning by exploring hypotheses goes a long way. Attending workshops that explore shifting paradigms may be helpful.

- Being more *conscientious* is likely more difficult to change than the other traits; improving it can be associated with having served in the military, and following orders and a specific schedule for a long period are bound to make you conscientious. Short of employing only ex-military, we can introduce self-discipline with standardized work for managers, problem solving with a PDCA loop, good workplace organization (5S) within the leadership's domain, and so on.

- Becoming more *extroverted* derives from more of a social aspect, although there are many encouraging benefits in the workplace, like increased customer contact, more professional opportunities, a focus on the greater good of the business instead of a focus on yourself. To become an extrovert, you need to undertake associated activates like going places where there are groups of people, mingling, becoming interested in other peoples activities. Forcing yourself to start a conversation is one way, but you can also lead five-minute stand-up meetings, lead discussions based on visual management, go to where the work takes place (the *gemba*) and ask question to transform yourself into an extravert. In other words, try to minimize email and other impersonal communication when it is imperative to witness someone's response and interact with or coach him or her.

- Balancing the team with more *agreeableness* begins by realizing that not everyone thinks and feels like you do, and that this is a normal phenomenon. Not recognizing different thinking and feelings is normally the basis for conflict and arguments; instead, you need to understand how people think, even the most difficult of those people. Try to imagine what is important to them, almost getting inside their heads and grasping their point of view, remember that decisions are made between the ears. If you can treat others by first understanding their priorities, then more or less "do onto others as you want them to do unto you," you will allow yourself to be more patient and compassionate and arrive at better decisions. I have found that by mentally tracking how often you find yourself in conflict with someone versus how often you took the time to try and get inside and understand his or her concerns, your awareness will be heightened, which should help you change, over the longer term. Also you can learn to read body language (and consider your body language) with training and books on subliminal communication. This will be discussed as nonverbal signals in Chapter 9. Understanding when it is appropriate to use intuitive thinking versus the need to utilize analytical methods also helps in reducing the conflicts associated with disagreeable people. Structured mentoring like that used in A3 Problem Solving and coaching or leadership techniques will also help in improving this trait; these will be discussed in more detail in Chapters 8 through 10. It is especially important to take care in trying to achieve a balanced score on agreeableness within your organization as those who score lower on agreeableness tend not to shy away from competition; they tend to push for outcome-driven results and challenge thoughts and opinions. You need this well balanced between those who score high and low in agreeableness; you can't have everyone agreeing, but you also can't have everyone pushing and challenging.

- Finally *neuroticism (emotional instability),* associated with pessimists, constitutes a tough way to go through life. By understanding that part of your brain is responsible for this trait and also knowing that others have successfully improved to become more optimistic, you may be able to get you started on improvement. If you work to become more extraverted, you should naturally become less pessimistic. By changing behavior in our work environment, we can have a positive impact. Celebrating success and rewarding people publically are a few of the ways to go about this. Extroversion and happiness can also be encouraged through after work activities and social clubs. Activities, hobbies, and socializing are all proven tactics to develop more emotionally stable people.

Being a pragmatic person, I like sticking to the more physical actions associated when working to change personality traits. But there are methodologies that use visualization (within your imagination) as a technique to create new behavioral patterns in the brain and these, in turn, change your personality traits. If you are interested in this route, you may want to research what has worked.

Possible Actions/Solutions for Decision-Making Traits

The DISC (dominance, influence, steadiness, compliance) personality assessment, the ROPELOC factors of personal effectiveness, and the Myers-Briggs Type Indicator focus on how you make decisions and work within a team. From the results of these self-assessments, you can determine where to focus in this next section.

First look at how you can improve departmental teamwork to help in arriving at better decisions. Some of these ideas likely should be included in your Cultural Transformation Plan. Your objective is always a balanced work team (I am referring to your department or daily working team, not project teams, although the same ideas apply). You need a balance between the traits, which were quantified in the results of these various assessments. You also need some team members to see the bigger picture, while others work through the details. It is quite natural within a group that certain people will assume different roles, although you need to make sure all your bases are covered; for example, if you have a room dominated by experts, but they do not see the entire picture, you are likely to experience frustration. On the other hand, if all have the same weaknesses, you have a weak team. If all have the same strengths, you are likely to have infighting and limited cooperation. So within a departmental team, you need motivators, implementers, coordinators, workers, analysts, and so on. Extroverts predominately have a preference for team-based cultures; therefore, you need to ensure we have sufficient extroverts to ensure strong teams within your culture.

In this way, assessments can be used to help you qualify two items in your cultural transformation:

- Are there any overly dominant team traits?

- Which team traits are missing?

In either case, you need to determine how to balance the situation, as you are unlikely to meet your objectives with a weak or unbalanced team. Another consideration is whether the leader is overwhelmed and stressed when working with his/her team and finds that a lot of non-productive time is leading to many extra working hours.

Other team improvement areas, which will again incorporate lean methodologies and tools, are:

- **Create a motivating environment.** A positive, optimistic leader that treats the team with respect goes a long way. Demonstrating courage and humility when leading (which are part of Chapter 9's topic: leading without power) go a long way in improving teamwork. Observing poor communication, negative body language, or undesirable expressions and making members aware is another key leadership/coaching responsibility. Also, taking time to socialize at lunch and other appropriate times puts the team at ease and creates more honesty within the group. Taking a leadership or coaching class will help further evolve this.

- **Lead from a *powerless* position.** Don't manage; instead lead by working with the team and mentoring them to become better problem solvers. Ensure time is available (away from the day-to-day firefighting) to work on improving processes.

- **Deal with negative people.** Don't let their poor attitude slide because they get the job done. Let them know that they drag down the other positive team members and that there are no exceptions. If necessary, deal with it at a performance or disciplinary level and encourage them to look elsewhere for an atmosphere where they will be happy (for everyone's sake).

- **Hold the team accountable.** Give them responsibility (once they are trained and skilled), and then hold them accountable. If you are uncomfortable confronting people, take some training on conflict management, or read books like Verbal Judo by George Thompson. It helps reduce overall confrontation and improves productivity and teamwork. Leaders feel more in control and can predict and neutralize situations to avoid hostility.

If the assessments indicate you are weak in some of the traits necessary for decision-making (like active involvement, open thinking, self confidence, coping with change, compliance, or an introverted personality), a few ideas and tools are mentioned here. Improving your ability in decision-making is a big subject, so I introduce only a few techniques that might be worthwhile to try if your analysis shows this as a weakness.

There are many decision-making models that can help add structure, but a few practical tools I often encourage organizations to pursue are:

- Learning to write and think in a business case format. Just type "writing a business case" into a search engine, and you'll find examples of what I am speaking about. This forces people to consider what leadership must reflect on when making a decision (i.e. return on investment) and requires you to be analytical. So consider training in this area.

- Stepladder technique for group decision-making. Everyone is encouraged to contribute (brainstorm) on an individual level before being influence by others. Handing out Post-its for everyone to individually write their ideas, gets a little skin in the game from the entire team. This allows the quiet and shy to get their ideas out without being stepped on by the louder more dominant part of the group.

- Awareness of analytical evaluation methods, exposure, and training on decision trees or grids, Pareto analysis, futures wheel, 5-whys, Ishikawa diagrams, and so on.

- Doing feedback analysis. This entails noting your hypotheses (over a year or two), and then 6 or 12 months after forming each theory, you compare it to the results and see what you can learn about your decision making.

- When to use intuitive versus analytical thinking. This critical subject that affects all of your decision-making will be explored in more detail in Chapter 8, where improvement suggestions will be offered.

Evaluating Open versus Closed Mindset

One other desirable trait previously mentioned is moving toward having an open mindset. An open mindset is associated with openness to growth and learning and believing in continuous improvement. This is in contradiction to the closed mindset that everyone possesses (at least partially) that suggests natural talents and abilities predetermine success.

Dr. Maynard Brusman[16] presents four simple mindsets to test where you sit. This is an ideal point in your Cultural Transformation Plan to also evaluate where you stand on this in relation to your desired culture.

You need to choose which mindset you have about your own intelligence:

1. Your intelligence is something very basic that cannot change much.

2. You can learn new things, but you can't really change how intelligent you are.

3. No matter how intelligent you are, you can always improve.

4. You can substantially change how intelligent you are.

If you chose either statement 1 or 2, this reflects a closed mindset, although statement 3 and 4 demonstrate an open mindset. Open-minded people take in feedback and improve themselves and their organizations, closed minds prefer filtered information so they only hear good news and do not improve. After determining where you fall, you should compare this to your desired cultural objectives, which likely involve an open mindset. You then need to consider which actions can help in changing your behavior toward continuously learning.

Committing to a Plan (Awareness/Analysis and Planned Actions)

If you've made it this far, it is time to compare your analysis (self-assessment results) to your objectives, factor in some of the previous improvement suggestions, and commit to a plan on paper. Some plan is better than no plan, and Post-its on large white paper are flexible, yet still represent a commitment to start some action. This transparent planning for each person shows respect and sets expectations. Vague discussions and plans make people uncomfortable, and they work less effectively.

This plan is what I have been referring to as your Cultural Transformation Plan, and it should support your strategy-deployment matrix. At this point, you should have started identifying areas to attack (on Post-its) and put those across the top header of the Cultural Transformation Plan (beginning to create the awareness/analysis row of a matrix, refer to Step 2 in Figure 6.1, which you began creating based on Chapter 6). In this top row, try to identify more of the behavioral issues you are trying to change—the specific actions that will be noted in the planning area of the Cultural Transformation Plan (become the body of the matrix: see Step 3 in Figure 6.1). Often it is hard not to jump to an action, although since the soft issues you are trying to resolve may be a bit gray, you require as much clarity and flexibility as possible. Wherever possible, distinguish what personality trait you are trying to change, and then it will be easier to define tangible actions.

I have found it best if you do this at a personal level or a position level instead of a general level. In other words, it is ideal to build a row for each person in the Cultural Transformation Plan and display these together as demonstrated in Figure 6.1. It should be based on knowledge of personal traits and behaviors along with the analysis (at least the parts in which you are in agreement based on the self-assessments). You should also be ready to plan some specific actions, tools, and trainings in the planning area (refer to in Step 3 of Figure 6.1). Remember that the format of the Cultural Transformation Plan is not important, except that it should encourage you to capture points of awareness in your organization in respect to your defined behavioral objectives, and then allow you to question what actions each leader could undertake. You might have the entire plan divided and visualized in separate areas, for example, one for each value stream and a separate visual for top leaders and functions.

The Plan (posting tangible actions in the body of the matrix in Figure 6.1) begins with the first tangible activity you can identify. To improve traits and behaviors, you will begin by gaining more in-depth knowledge on this trait or concept, so that you become more convinced of how you can go about changing it. Training, a workshop, or some other external experience may be necessary in this regard.

After increasing your knowledge and conviction toward the importance of changing this behavior, you are likely to identify the next step, which will usually involve modifying an on-going behavior and some form of monitoring. For example, you might take a course on shifting your paradigm (in response to developing more cutting edge products) and determine that you require more time in the field, with customers utilizing the current technology at its upper limits. Naturally, the Post-its you place in the planning cells should address the points of analysis you captured in the awareness/analysis row (refer to Figure 6.1).

All the points introduced in this section 'Committing to a Plan', also are derived from the work being done at the value stream level in both Figures 6.2 and 7.1. You need to decide at the company level whether you want to visualize the plan in its entirety or rather visualize and manage at the value stream levels. You might develop a format that contains the actions identified in Figure 7.1 for each value stream and work from there. Likely you will need some format to document the discoveries and plans for the top leaders, including any actions for the company wide issues like changing to a flatter structure, office layouts, dress codes, etc. The point is, don't adopt it, but adapt it, the book is only sharing what others have done and providing a structure to begin your own experimentation.

Identifying and Reshaping Habits

One of the typical actions to be undertaken is the reshaping of habits. Reshaping is easier than creating new habits, so where you identify a behavior (that is actually a habit) which is not desirable, or you are trying to create some new habits, you need a basic understanding of how they function and the best way to alter them. Although habits are more flexible during a crisis, lets focus on improving habits as part of continuous improvement or for reaching breakthroughs. Now I will briefly discuss how habits work within an organization, but I encourage you to explore this in more depth. There are the cases like Alcoa, which experienced vast improvements when Paul O'Neill came on board as the new CEO and reshaped many of the organization's habits. Though you will also find many examples of how habits are reshaped without introducing new leadership, one book that is highly recommended is: The Power of Habit by Charles Duhigg.

Our brains will attempt to make any routine into a habit, as this requires less effort from the brain, a form of autopilot. A habit follows a simple loop consisting of three components, first is the *cue*, and then comes the *routine* followed by the *reward*. *Cues* can be almost anything, they can be very simple or more complex, it could be a certain time of the day, triggered by an emotion, triggered by an event, or prompted by certain people. The *routine* does not have to be physical, it can be an emotional or mental. The *reward* must be memorable; it can be anything from satisfying a craving to accomplishing a necessary task. Habits can develop outside someone's consciousness or be intentionally developed, though in either case they can be reshaped.

So lets imagine as your team identifies desirable behaviors (the methodology detailed in chapters 6 and 7), and that someone becomes aware he/she doesn't possess an important trait or behavior, a solution might be to alter the routine of an existing habit, or try creating a new one. This is actually easier to apply in the workplace as you have teammates that can support you and likely require the same habit in meeting their objectives. So first you need to identify an easy and obvious cue, next you must clarify the rewards and alter or develop the routine.

For personal habits you need to create a sense of craving (the reward), and although the same is true in the workplace, often you first need to develop a belief in the reward, for example, creating an awareness that the habit will help achieve an objective or resolve a problem. When changing a habit, often the cue and reward stay the same and the routine is changed. Getting rid of bad habits is also difficult as they are driven by cues and rewards, so it is better to try and change the routine than trying to eliminate the habit. An example could be when someone openly disagrees with you, your previous routine might have been to raise your voice and quickly give an angry reply, the new routine might be to meditate for a moment before answering in anger.

What is important is that by better understanding habits and the cues, along with the cravings and rewards that drive them, we have a better chance to alter them in the direction of meeting the objectives. Again this can be easier in the work place if the entire team is working to improve the culture as you can support each other in changing habits. Often a workplace routine is part of a group routine. Naturally changing certain habits will be part of the actions discovered when developing your Cultural Transformation Plan; therefore you must become familiar in how to recognize habits. What has been demonstrated in organizations is changing some fundamental habits leads to other benefits. A bad habit I often observe, that if countered with a good habit, leads to many other benefits is when people are checking their smartphones during discussions or meetings. If you can turn that cue (the craving to constantly check messages) into a routine of better listening behaviors (explained in chapter 9) the reward will be improved leadership. An example of a good habit within a continuous improvement journey that leads to other desirable habits is workplace organization (known as 5S to lean practitioners). This creates structure and a small win that leads to other benefits and habits. Other examples of habits that lead to additional benefits are: Gemba walks, getting in the habit of exposing problems, stand-up meetings (improvements include better organization and time management), being punctual, etc. You can even reduce the undesirable impact of a leadership's behaviors when competing for power or taking credit, by putting in place certain habits of recognizing other's efforts through rewards.

A great example of introducing cornerstone habits that drove an organization's success was when Alcoa appointed Paul O'Neill their new CEO in an effort to turn around the company's growth and profitability. He focused on instilling new habits to improve their safety record, to the concern of many stakeholders preoccupied with profitability. What he knew was by changing habits relating to safety within Alcoa's plants, many other good habits would result thereby increasing productivity, reducing tensions and gaining buy-in to name a few. It turned out to be one of the great corporate turnarounds, based on changing some key habits that many did not recognize for their true value.

Further research on improving habits will demonstrate they are a cornerstone for sales and marketing processes. Companies like Starbucks Coffee train their staff to cue in on angry customers or coworkers and then develop positive routines so the reward is a happy customer. The key is always to believe that the change is feasible, and link the new routine to the existing cues and rewards. Creating this belief usually requires the help of a group; therefore its success is more likely when it is a conscious effort in the transformation plan.

Summary

Ideally, you should now have an annual strategy-deployment matrix that incorporates a process of continuous follow-up and adjustment. Awareness of the need to transform the culture should be understood and supported by top leadership; behavioral objectives for the cultural part of the transformation should be developed. For each desired trait identified by the value stream teams, they should brainstorm how an individual can create awareness of their current state for that desired behavior (including the use of personality assessments), and what actions they could take to improve it (i.e. developing Figure 7.1). Top leadership's personality assessments should have been checked for misalignments with the objectives, specifically for the traits of agreeableness and neuroticism (these are the two areas where it has been scientifically demonstrated that CEOs have the strongest influence on the culture). If it is felt any shortcomings cannot be overcome, the strategic objectives should be reconsidered. If all is okay, then you move on to the personality assessments identified as applicable for the remaining leadership team (usually through to the team leader level). Once you have those results, this chapter should help in identifying areas of improvement and specific activities that should lead us toward achieving our new culture. These shortcomings that we feel can be overcome should be noted in the Awareness/Analysis row, and the actions or tools to achieve this should be proposed in the Planning cells of the Cultural Transformation Plan. Having the entire leadership team engaged in defining your developmental process (and vice-versa) should help change the perceptions you have of each other.

Figure 7.2 summarizes the steps you have undertaken to this point.

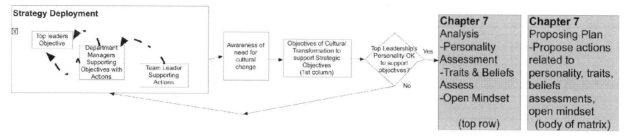

Figure 7.2: Process Steps through Chapter 7

By starting this awareness and self-assessment process, you should be working toward enlightening yourself in the following manners:

- Clarifying your current leadership style and behaviors

- Start working to improve interpersonal relationships

- Broaden your perspective on the effects of the soft issues

- Becoming a better learner

- Becoming a better leader

In Chapter 8, we further explore decision-making by understanding and evaluating when we should use either intuitive or analytical thinking as the basis for our judgments. All subsequent chapters suggest practical ideas to move your culture toward your desired traits and behaviors, and these ideas will be incorporated as you continue refining your Cultural Transformation Plan.

CHAPTER 8

Intuitive versus Analytical Thinking

Creating a Cultural Transformation Plan requires a partial understanding of the silent and automatic parts of our mind in relation to decision-making. We need to gain an insight into intuitive thinking (our gut feel). Changing a culture involves changing how determinations are made, and in this arena, your mentality plays a key role.

This chapter will help to:

- Understand the power and dangers of intuitive thinking

- Improve your ability to recognize situations where your biases could lead to errors in decisions

- Improve your ability to recognize situations where other's biases could lead to poor decisions

- Combine intuitive and analytical thinking, since decision makers are facing additional pressure for quick decisions in your more turbulent and complex environments

- Clarify how both Intuitive and Analytical Thinking affect your transformation plan

Defining Intuitive and Analytical Thinking

Intuition can be described as "thoughts and preferences that come to mind quickly and without much reflection,"[17] and you can look at this as acting on a hunch or emotions. Intuitive thoughts are fast, they are usually based on recognition of either a behavior or an experience. This is a painless and quick way to make a decision, the bad news is it often ignores data and does not consider new information. It creates beliefs that we cannot usually rationalize with facts, which can lead to some dangerous business conclusions. Intuitive thinking can be broken into our normal intuition we utilize each day and expert intuition, which many feel is the value they contribute to the organization. I want to extend our discussion equally to the daily and expert intuition as they both apply in the working environment.

Analytical thinking is at the opposite end of the scale; it can be considered logical, factual, critical, quantitative, and is usually also technical. It will include specifically defining the problem, gathering data, analyzing, understanding, evaluating ideas (based on facts), and so on. Naturally this is a longer and slower process, and for most people it is painful (measured through increased stress and eye pupil dilation). We need both intuitive and analytical thinking in our organizations; the trick is to balance the available decision time and the decisions implications between the fast intuitive and the slow analytical judgments.

Why Is Intuitive versus Analytical Thinking Important?

We all have beliefs and make judgments that lead to errors in our choices, understanding and grouping these errors is easier to do with other people and more difficult to identify in ourselves. After reading this chapter you should have a better handle on how to go about identifying mistakes in your choices as well as with your teammates, and ideas how you can improve your own decision-making and influence your teams thinking in this area.

In considering the daily choices each of us faces regarding decision-making (or problem solving), you can visualize the process using Figure 8.1.

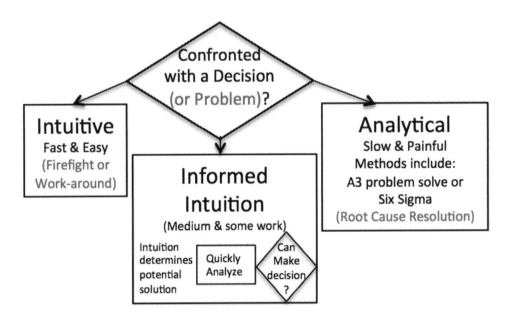

Figure 8.1 Beginning of the Decision-Making Process

Often without much thought we choose the intuitive route, periodically we decide on 'informed intuition' (defined later in this chapter) and less frequently we complete a full analysis. How this decision is made and how it affects the outcome are some of the considerations to be discussed. Of great interest should be the knowledge of how often you are right or wrong and which types of decisions you are best at (as applied to your working environment).

Figure 8.1 can also be applied when we are presented with a problem, the intuitive direction is similar to choosing to implement a work-around or firefight the problem, as opposed to the analytical method where you invest the time for permanently resolving the issue at its root cause. We tend to have norms or habits that take us in one direction or another; therefore we need to understand our tendencies and how often they lead to the right decision. It is not often a single habit or behavior determines how we make a decision, but it's typical for a combination of our habits, processes and behaviors to move us in a particular direction.

As more time pressure enters our working world, it appears there is less time available for any analysis; therefore, decision makers are continually being pushed toward more intuitive decision-making (as it results in fast decisions). We need to take this into account in our planning for the new culture, especially in these rapidly changing, less predictable environments. Both our intuitive thinking and our environment are now being radically affected by the readily available information on the Internet, often influencing how we go about making decisions.

Your daily intuitive thoughts affect both your personal and working lives. We all see through a different set of eyes and all of our intuitions differ. Let's start with examples from your personal lives that apply directly into our working lives, for instance, when calling your spouse you might recognize anger in their tone and you likely make the immediate decision to proceed with caution or ask what's wrong. Or you observe an acquaintance walking fast with his head down and recognize he is in deep thought and does not want to be interrupted for casual conversation.

At work, these same situations might manifest themselves when calling a client, and you recognize by the client's tone that she is unhappy, or you see a colleague is walking fast and purposefully in the hallway and recognize he is very busy and does not have time to answer a quick question. These are your very basic intuitions and will not be a major consideration in this book other than your cultural transformation should take into account if someone is lacking certain daily intuitions, because this will lead to undesirable behaviors and decisions. In either case, consider awareness training, new organizational structures, changing a team's layout, new meeting formats, and the like, all of which can help offset any negative impact.

Our beliefs are constantly changing as we acquire new knowledge and experiences, this is a reason lean thinking encourages going to *gemba* (the real place where value is created) to see for yourself. Interestingly, we often forget our former beliefs as new knowledge moves us toward a new belief. To understand the importance of this in your organizational environment, let's take a simple example with respect to lean implementation: someone was part of a company that started on a lean journey utilizing the tools approach, but then had a bad experience as the tools were incorrectly focused at aggressive productivity improvements and they overloaded the worker (in Toyota terms, this is *muri,* or overburden). It is important to understand the impression created about lean, because the individual's intuition is to stay away from lean. But all is not lost, because if you can prove a positive lean effect through new knowledge and experiences, the former belief will be disregarded and replaced with the newer and more positive belief.

Impressions and intuitions lead to decisions; these are all based on beliefs formed from knowledge and experience. Leaders can get a grasp on guidance in the course of having a better understanding of these relationships and applying it in the work setting. It is also critical to understand your intuitions as well as other's intuitions when mentoring, and since coaching and utilizing A3 Problem Solving are both forms of mentoring encouraged in this book (and likely part of your Cultural Transformation Plan), this understanding is crucial. The understanding of biases and how they affect people's intuition is also critical when assessing your current cultures and subcultures, as discussed in Chapter 6.

Bottom line: you need awareness and consideration of the various bias's that influence your beliefs and decisions. Without becoming a psychologist, consider if some of these are easily identifiable for the layman, and how this knowledge could be advantageous. An example of naming a bias could be the *halo effect;* it is possible you have this bias toward me while reading this book, because I have been established as a subject-matter expert, and that has a certain expectation in your mind. By establishing myself as an expert, you might be *more* biased in accepting my experiences and suggestions (this is the halo effect), although just by having a name and creating awareness, you are less susceptible to this bias and more likely to judge the information a bit more critically. Therefore, creating a name for various biases helps you to recognize them and minimize their impact, reducing errors in decision-making.

When Is Expert Intuitive Thinking a Risk?

Expert Intuitive Thinking is when someone is considered a specialist, utilizing his or her skill and experience to make a recommendation without having completed an analysis (its possible there was no data available). This is something we gravitate towards, especially as our increasingly complex world requires more expertise to navigate. Here, consider when this can become more of a liability then a desired attribute in the organization. Expert intuition is something that has varying degrees of importance depending on the type of business. Many service companies primary product is some form of expertise. For example, financial, investment services, law firms, and design companies are often selling a combination of experience and analysis. Much of the experience and analyzing of the data is grounded in the intuitive thoughts of the experts. The same applies for many manufacturers. Take, for example, technical products or precision products: they are selling their expertise, residing in either experience, or from having the right intuitive thinkers on the team. Though even if you are not necessarily an *expert*, but instead have more analytical traits, others will come to expect you to perform the analytical thinking.

What you need to recognize is that expert intuitive decisions in *unpredictable* situations are often wrong. This is not true when applying expert intuition to orderly situations (i.e. medical situations, technical situations), because intuition is fundamentally correct in these environments. But experts who claim to have intuition in erratic situations/environments have been shown to obtain worse results than would have been achieved through random guesses (with random probability). A 20-year study by Philip Tetlock[18] involved 284 experts (making a living "commenting or offering advice on political and economic trends,") and 82,361 predictions, he grouped most questions into 3 possible answers so they could be statistically measured. The experts performed worse than they would have if they had simply assigned an equal probability to all three outcomes. In other words the experts are not statistically better predictors of the future than you or me in these unpredictable environments. And because their livelihood is based on it, when they're wrong, they rarely admit it, and are rarely held accountable.

How do these interesting facts affect your organization? It tells us to be careful using too much expert opinion (which is often intuitive) when making decisions around an unpredictable future. That implies we want to be analytical as often as possible and when time permits or the effort will justify the reward. Now, these experts will not want to hear how their prediction rates are lower than random guessing, as they feel threatened. If you are to show an expert data demonstrating very low correlations of choosing the right outcome, you are indicating they are not as valuable as they perceive themselves to be, and there is likely a lot of luck involved when they do get it right. In cases when experts have been presented with data demonstrating that their predictions are often wrong (most applicably in the financial world), they might accept the data on an intellectual level, but often it will not impact future actions. What can they do if their livelihood is based on their expert opinion? They must create a psychological illusion to continue with utilizing their skills to make a living.

Aside from the proven dangerous of using expert's intuition in politics, economics, and picking stocks; within your organization, examples of where you might use caution would be trusting the sales and marketing's expert intuition in the following areas:

- Sales projections for new product introduction

- Future customer preferences

- General market and sales intuition

Those are probably some fairly obvious examples, although the recommended action is creating a feedback loop to prove to yourself how valid expert intuition is in your situation. By this I mean to track hypotheses against the actual results and try to become more of a learning organization through reflection. I cannot recall, when supporting organizations, the last time I encountered one that had a robust tracking, reflecting, and learning system for their sales and marketing projections. In fairness, often you will not be able to draw conclusions because of the un-predictableness of the events you encounter, but a feedback system will provide two benefits:

- Periodically, you will identify something you overlooked and can take it into account in the future (possibly developing checklists for future decision-making)

- Those experts will realize their intuitions cannot necessarily be trusted and become more inclined to consider if the slower and painful analytical method should instead be utilized to improve the decision-making.

Intuitive thinking is not bad or wrong; it's necessary and will always be the dominant guide for your decisions. It can help you to swerve your car around a dangerous object at the last moment; it also is necessary to take over in emergency situations. Although in your professional life it is necessary to understand when you may want to use either the more painful and slow form of analytical thinking, or pure intuitive thought, or some combination of intuitive and analytical thinking. We also want to recognize when intuitive thinking is affecting the decisions of people in our organization, and consider how we might be able to influence it. Determining and separating predictable from less predictable environments is one step, although you know certain areas where there are no other options, try to imagine the medical field without expert intuition—in more regular and predictable environments it is of great value. Consider defaulting to rules for complicated decisions when short on time, and you are likely to minimize errors.

Deciding When Analytical thinking Is Necessary

First a question: If together a hamburger and French-fries cost $2.50, and the hamburger costs $2.00 more than the French-fries, how much do the French-fries cost? You should determine your answer before continuing to read.

If you answered fifty cents, you are thinking fast and intuitively and, unfortunately, you are wrong. The correct answer is the French-fries cost twenty-five cents. The hamburger (which costs two dollars *more* than the French-fries) would cost two dollars and twenty-five cents, plus the twenty-five cents for the french-fries, giving you a total of two dollars and fifty cents.

This is a quick example of how comfortable, quick, and sometimes lazy we are with intuitive thought. What's important to recognize is when this can lead to poor business decisions. Intuition can frequently be even more dangerous, as it is affected by our moods; for example, when you are happy, you let your guard down; when you are unhappy, you are less likely to use intuition to quickly decide something.

When switching to analytical thinking, increased levels of stress have been measured; pupil dilations have also been observed and are correlated to the anticipated painfulness of this process. This is likely because any analysis requires effort and natural laziness leads to avoiding this.

When is intuitive thought okay in the work place?

- If an error in judgment is not too costly, you might jump to a quick decision.

- If the potential error will be discovered before delivery to the customer.

- If the situation is very familiar to one in the past.

- If it happens automatically, cannot be turned off, and time is not available for analytical thinking.

So when might we consider analytical thinking necessary:

- If the wrong decision could be costly.

- If it could affect the customer.

- In unfamiliar situations.

- If you feel you have too little information to make a decision.

- If you have a history of incorrect predictions (determined through feedback analysis).

- If popular thinking is pushing the team into thinking with a mob mentality.

An additional consideration in making analytical work more pleasant and rapid is what has become known as *"Information Excellence"*, a method to collect, analyze and act upon data in the most effective way possible. Most data is backwards looking and continues to be reported in the same formats limiting its decision-making value. Most manufacturing companies underutilize the wealth of available information/knowledge as they do not have a system to manage large sets of data. So company wide data-management/analysis systems can be developed by deciding what data to collect and more importantly why it is being collected (i.e. only to measure past performance). This results in easy access to the correct data with effective formats, being acted upon by the right people with an understanding of how to utilize this in forward looking decisions. Remember we want push decision-making responsibility to those closest to the value adding processes. You might want to familiarize yourself with how *Information Excellence* thinking can help.

Cultural Change Affected by the Style of Decision-Making

How does your style of decision-making affect your cultural change or lean thinking? For instance, it is often determined that the new culture needs to expose and resolve more problems, it needs to move the responsibility for decision-making to the lowest levels, we want leaders not managers, and so on. A critical cultural change is we need to encourage the exposure of problems (remember remarking you have "no problems" exposes a major problem in your mentality). The assumption in many cultural changes is that problem solving (i.e. analytical thinking) will be more in demand to address the additional problems being exposed. The underlying assumptions are also that leadership will consciously choose analysis instead of intuitively trying to make a decision, but you likely need more than just encouraging the exposure of problems to influence which direction you take in your on-going decision-making (Figure 8.1).

In lean journeys, we often focus on leadership's responsibility in problem solving. This is highlighted in lean journeys through mentoring methods like A3 Problem Solving, although you must first make a conscious decision that a problem requires analytical thinking before considering which method to use. Please don't misunderstand, I believe A3 Problem Solving is a critical part of a cultural change and everyone should be familiar with its importance. It's just that you need to recognize when its required and put forth the effort to utilize it. I cannot offer any pragmatic solution in the case of deciding when you must switch to the slower analytical route, but one way to draw some of your own conclusions is to utilize the feedback analysis that was previously introduced. This is where you write down your hypotheses that were derived intuitively, and months later match them to the actual results, this should help you access how often you might want to stop and perform analysis. Once you decide on analysis, then lean problem solving like A3 or six sigma (for more complicated technical problems) are most applicable.

Finding the Balance for Your New Culture

A balance of intuitive and analytical thinking is necessary, we can call this *informed intuition*, although before discussing why this is most appropriate, let's look at the extremes. Some telltale signs that can lead to using too much intuitive thinking:

- You are almost never stumped (i.e. you have an answer for everything)

- Not even noticing the difficulty of a question

- Being given very little information and easily accepting a statement as true

- Suppressing doubt and ambiguity

Some telltale signs that intuition is practical:

- Little time available

- Lots of uncertainty exists

- Little or no previous experience exist

- Variables have little scientific predictability

- Little data is available

- Not enough time to digest all the available data

You just need to be aware of the dangers of only using intuitive thoughts, although there might be no choice other than instinct.

The best alternative, assuming there is the option for some analysis, is probably two fold: first you need to understand any biases that limit the accuracy of intuitive decision-making, for example:

- **Confirming bias:** looking for information that agrees with your thinking and avoiding contrary information, as we are always more motivated by positives rather than by negatives

- **Anchoring bias:** when we put a lot more weight on the first information we come across

- **Want-ability bias:** this is allowing a strong desire to outweigh any discussions or analysis to the contrary

Second, you need to change from only intuitive thinking to *informed Intuition*, meaning you look for evidence to back up your intuitive thoughts. Naturally this can only be based on the analysis of available data, but it circumvents many of the dangers of pure intuitive decision-making. In other words, intuitive and analytical are not exclusive, but are complementary, and when the decision is needed as quickly as possible, it carries some risk. Working together, you encounter medium speed and improved accuracy, likely the best combination. This can be performed as either more of a single-step or a multi-step process: a single step is when intuition tells you to search for data (perform analysis) and you do this loop 1X and are content to make a decision, or *multi-step informed intuition,* where you do the loop multiple times because after receiving the initial data, your intuition tells you to look further into the facts or move in another direction. Naturally a one-loop process is faster than multiple loops, although depending on time versus the consequences the decision carries, you will have to choose.

Therefore, first try to recognize and categorize your biases, because this awareness improves your intuitive decision-making, and if you are to then take that intuition and seek concrete evidence, you are using *informed-intuition*, which should be fast enough (usually quicker than completely launching an analytical analysis), and will achieve more accurate results than pure intuition. This middle-of-the-road solution is likely the most practical in your fast-paced turbulent global environment. Case in point would be DuPont, which reduced its product-development cycle from three years to just about three months by combing intuitive thinking into its very-analytical product planning team (*DuPont's Interactive Planning Process*).[19]

Presentation of Information Affects Decision-making

How information is relayed can often affect where you focus, which in turn influences your intuitive decision-making. We'll discuss only two examples within this area, although there are many. First let's look at *loss aversion*: this takes place when evaluating gains and losses, with losses always taking precedence over gains. This is not surprising, and a good example is observed when renegotiating contracts. We often use the current terms and conditions as a reference point, and any time we give away something (based on the current terms), it appears as a loss; this then becomes a bigger issue then the potential gain in the overall negotiation. We naturally fight harder to prevent a loss then protect a gain. Another illustration is that bad things always take precedence over good things. We might decide to continue with a losing project instead of admitting failure and chalking up a loss on our record. It is important to recognize how this can be used as an advantage or a disadvantage (against you) in forming a decision. A final example is that retaining long-term customers depends more on avoiding negatives (loss aversion) that on seeking positives. This is a reason lean implementation focuses first on customer quality.

The second example to discuss is the *format, emphasis, or order* in which information is presented. For example, I started this book trying to grab your attention by stating, "two-thirds of lean transformations fail to achieve sustainable results." I could have said one-third of lean journeys are successful, but I wanted you to focus on failures and continue reading. Another example would be to say that 1 in 1,000 die from a certain drug, the intention is you are to focus on the 1 and consider you could become that 1 person, versus stating that 99.9 percent have no adverse affects. I think the desired effect is obvious, although you need to be aware so this does not bias your intuitive decision-making.

Many industries market to our fears; they are hoping your intuitive thinking is the only consideration, with no time is taken for analysis. Insurance companies like to present data in such a manner that you buy more insurance; they play on peace of mind. They might over-estimate probabilities of unlikely events, pushing the human intuitive system to consider purchasing more insurance.

Transforming Ideas Into Your Cultural Transformation Plan

It is a good time to consider how intuitive and analytical decision-making might translate into your Cultural Transformation Plan. It is likely you would consider adding some of the following suggestions into the Awareness/Analysis row (Step 2 in Figure 6.1).

- Priming ideas helps implant intuitive thoughts toward gaining acceptance

- Creating awareness in culture to focus on predictable biases in ourselves and others (usually easier to observe and prevent errors with others, than in ourselves)

- Tracking the frequency of informed intuition versus analytical thinking being utilized in your decision-making.

In the planning cells (Step 3 in Figure 6.1), where you are converting traits and behaviors into the beginnings of tangible actions, you might include:

- Feedback analysis (hypotheses compared to actual results over a period of time)

- Training on how to better recognize various biases in ourselves and others

- Creating checklists, so that a consideration in decision-making is not forgotten

- Recognizing any basic deficiencies in daily decision-making within the team, which could lead to actions such as reorganizing the team, organization restructuring, and a new seating layout.

- Determining where someone needs to experience a positive change based on a previous belief ascertained through a negative experience in that area, so the bias is removed by the positive experience and by his or her beliefs and intuition change

- With written messages, utilizing simple words, on nice paper using a plain font engages your lazy thinking and easier agreement; using difficult words and fonts invokes analytical thinking.

I am not aware of any self-assessments for intuitive versus analytical thinking. There are personality tests that help distinguish between intuitive and sensing personalities, but that is the extent to which an assessment tool could be used to create awareness.

Summary

Intuitive is fast automatic thinking, versus analytical, which is slow and requires effort. Intuitive will always be the foundation of what you do right and what you do wrong, it guides your actions, it will be most often accurate and that accuracy will be increased through experience and skills. Although you need to recognize that your intuition leads to wrong decisions, unfortunately you cannot make major changes with your intuition; the best you can do is improve your abilities in recognizing situations that will lead you into relying too heavily on your biases, resulting in errors of judgment. Preconceived notions are easier to observe in others, although as a leader, you want to increase your own skills in recognizing these circumstances in yourself. Unfortunately you are under more time pressure in rapidly changing and less predictable environments; therefore, you don't often have the luxury of time to perform the complete analysis that might minimize errors. Although you can curtail these errors by combining intuition with some analysis, often called *informed intuition* (Figure 8.1), which is likely the best solution.

This interdependency of intuitive and analytical thinking should be viewed as a reasonable solution to deal with this more turbulent and complex global environment. The process is referred to as informed intuition. Decision makers can provide background and general direction by utilizing their intuition and requesting that experts do the analysis. This might go back and forth as the decision maker reviews the data, and their intuition identifies that more or different data is required. This back and forth between intuition and analysis is still faster than pure in-depth analytical thinking, which usually incorporates a deeper investigation before reviewing the data.

Using feedback analysis (monitoring your hypothesis's against the results over a long period of time) should help in determining how much pure intuition, or informed intuition, or pure analytical thinking are required. The decision-making style you adapt will be based on a combination of the complexity of the problem, the type of decision, and the person making the decision. In your Cultural Transformation Plan, you likely want a high level of awareness between utilizing intuitive thinking and deciding on analytical thinking or choosing the middle ground of *informed intuition.* People's awareness and understanding of their styles and the concept of when they should use a particular type of thinking, will help in arriving at the best decisions.

To visualize how the discussion in this chapter fits into your overall cultural change, consider that you have been looking at what additional decision-making items are to be included in the Awareness/Analysis and Plan sections of your Cultural Transformation Plan, as highlighted in Figure 8.2.

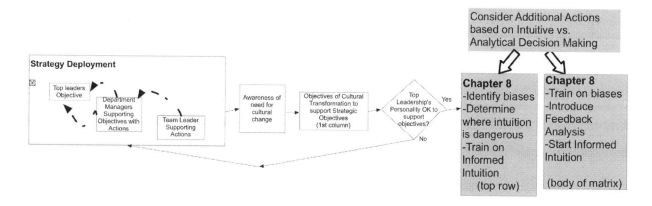

Figure 8.2 Process Steps through Chapter 8

In the next chapter, we will explore *leading without power,* which includes the leader's choice of words, listening abilities, and nonverbal signals The opportunities to become a better coach and mentor will also be opened to discussion, as this crucial aspect creates additional awareness and actions for the Cultural Transformation Plan to support your breakthrough objectives.

CHAPTER 9

Leading Without Power

To lead instead of manage people, you need to assume your position holds no power and instead convince people to move forward. It involves going to the real place where value is added *(gemba)* and learning what actually transpires, allowing you to develop respect for team members and the team respecting their leaders. Leadership is an earned gift from the team based on mutual respect. To accomplish this, we will look at a few additional factors to consider for your Cultural Transformation Plan; those are:

- Using the right language, words, and nonverbals

- Leaders listening effectively and empathizing

- Coaching and mentoring

Each will be discussed with the intent to evaluate your current situation and evaluate where your organization needs to focus to align with your desired cultural change. The resulting decisions can then be incorporated into your cultural transformation.

Although, historically, the importance of leadership and coaching was established centuries ago and reaffirmed during war times, empirical data demonstrating improved productivity and reduced grievances can be found in the 1945 War Production Board's report on the success of the Training Within Industry (TWI) program (reproduced in Appendix F). These results, including more than doubling productivity while cutting grievances in almost half, were achieved by implementing leadership skills for the supervision and middle-management levels, though more importantly, we need leadership change driven by the top leadership leading by example.

Leadership Is All About the Words

I've come across leaders with excellent technical knowledge while others possessed a profound understanding of their market and customers. Some appeared to have great visions for the organization, whereas others were so inspirational and compelling that I immediately wanted to work with them. Although no matter what talents they possess, the leader's tools are predominately their words. The context and connotation of using the right versus wrong words can separate successful and unsuccessful leaders. That said, I give you this word of caution: just because the leader's tools are his words, this doesn't mean he should be continuously talking. Too many words are more dangerous than too few. It is better to use a few precise and insightful words than to speak continuously, because other than boring your colleagues, you increase the risk of using the wrong words and giving the wrong message.

Communication is also very much a two-way street, likely the reason we have two ears and only one mouth! Great leaders are normally excellent public speakers, although listening creates the critical balance of being able to speak to the audience. Becoming a skilled listener is not easy, and many potential leaders are lacking in this area. It is a crucial skill in organizational leadership, which is why I have dedicated a section of this chapter to it, focusing specifically on how you can recognize a listening deficiency and improve your listening skills. This is likely another matter that deserves consideration in your Cultural Transformation Plan.

Let's begin with the words leaders use, as they have a greater impact than some might imagine. Barking out a quick order or voicing a judgment about someone, carries more weight than thought and might carry certain risks when coming from an inspiring and respected leader. The wrong word or something is said out of context can blow up, even if the negative effects are not immediately apparent. Leaders use speech to inspire, persuade, or update, yet the wrong choice of words can discourage, demoralize, anger, or confuse. The right words make the team feel valued, respected, and encouraged to work toward the betterment of the organization. The average speed with which people speak is between 110 and 150 words per minute, so imagine the swath of damage that can quickly spread from a leaders lack of awareness. An offhand comment can be taken as new policy within the organization, which means that every word is crucial.

Culture Is Defined by Words

Words also have an impact on the culture because leaders create opportunities and opinions with them. Now imagine the way you refer to customers, address co-workers, refer to people's jobs (that is, job titles) or address colleagues: these can all move the culture in either a progressive or regressive direction. Creating a successful culture comes down to what leaders and team members say. Just look at some of the words I am using that will help create loyalty and a constructive team environment; for example, throughout this book, I refer to people within the organization as team members, never employees. Naturally there are other terms, like associates, partners, or colleagues that also lead to a successful culture versus terms like subordinates or workers, which communicate an us versus them mentality, driving subcultures into the organization. This is only one illustration; this chapter will provide a list of predominate words that should not be used by leaders trying to create a lean culture.

Vision statements, slogans, or posters hanging in the lobby do not define culture; instead, it is really determined by what leaders and the team members say and how they say it. So part of the analysis of your existing culture should focus on the words used by leaders, as well as nonverbal signals given. This chapter includes a partial list of words and phrases that should not be utilized, and you can track over a day or week how often you hear these negative words. Are they coming from leaders or team members? After reading this and similar literature, your awareness should also be increased to the point of better evaluating the current nonverbal communication and listening skills within your company.

Can You Change Your Vocabulary?

Before simply stating that you must use a new vocabulary, as this involves changing your habits, consider how the entire process works so that you can better decide how to change it. Your thoughts become your words followed by your words turning into actions. Thoughts transforming into words transpire within a nanosecond; therefore, you need to slow down this process, as it is unrealistic to alter your subconscious in creating thoughts. You want to create a practice that allows you to slow down and reflect or meditate prior to speaking, and naturally this is easier if you are speaking less and listening more. You want your words to reflect your values; you need to realize that your anxiety and quick judgments can lead to nervously throwing out words without any thought. So you want to create a practice of noticing your thoughts as they arise and reflecting before you speak.

You also can affect your thoughts by focusing on any anger or negative feelings building up and reflect on how they will help serve your leadership. If you recognize any negativity or anger, force yourself to quickly meditate or take a second to reflect, your next words are likely to represent these negative thoughts and, although you might need to convey some of this negativity, it might serve better to ask questions and allow the self-realization from your colleagues to crystallize the reasons for the negativity or anger. Constructive coaching and encouragement are the other way to handle negative thoughts, as reprimanding someone publically only encourages sympathy for the victim and anger toward the leader.

So it boils down to changing your habits and to do this, you need to first convince yourself how often this transpires and consider the influence of our words. So as part of the Awareness/Analysis column in your Cultural Transformation Plan, evaluate yourself and other leaders as to the frequency in utilizing the right or wrong words, and then consider some of the recommendations in this chapter to begin working on tangible actions.

Words Not to Use

Let's look at some examples of the words and phrases that inspire, persuade, and create opportunities and opinions versus those that can discourage , demoralize, anger, or confuse us (see Figure 9.1). The context, connotation, and any non-verbals put forth when using words help frame the message that is communicated, although at this point we are looking only at the words and phrases themselves.

Sends Wrong Message	Sends Right Message
employees, subordinates, workers	team members, associates, partners, or colleagues
He's just an administrative assistant, I'm just the team leader	He has the responsibility as my administrate assistant, I fulfill all the responsibilities of a team leader
Deadlines, due dates, targets	Our goals, our targets, our customers, our results, our outcomes
I'll give you a chance	I know you can do it
coming in short, dropping the ball, botching the job	victory, achievement, performance, payoff
problem	situation or challenge
this will not work, You've got that wrong	we have to keep trying, You have gained experience
We can not afford mistakes	I've made a mistake
kind of, sort of	Six times last week, The data indicates
I know exactly what the problem is	What do you think the issue is?
no, but, however (to start a sentence)	Lets think about, Considering, I have a thought

Figure 9.1: Examples of the Right and Wrong Words

You can see how the right or wrong message can be sent through the examples in Figure 9.1. The list of right words is only a small sample but should help get you started in evaluating both yourself and the leadership in your organization.

Leaders must try to create positive images, even if the situation is dire. You want to encourage continuous improvement, learning, and risk-taking with your words. And when a difficult or disciplinary conversation is required, better to be direct, choosing your words carefully and focusing the discussion toward behaviors.

Recommendations for Changing the Words You Use

Remember that your words will be amplified and distorted as they move among the organization. My recommendation is to first evaluate the words being used, and then consider some of the following for the Plan column in your Cultural Transformation Plan.

- Take a coaching or mentoring class.

- Develop lists of the right words to use. These should be words that clarify, convey respect, encourage, relate to your audience, encourage optimism, raise challenging questions, encourage learning, and inspire.

- Identify all the wrong words you use and try self-tracking, as well as asking colleagues to track each time you use those words.

- Work to take a moment to reflect (meditate) before speaking

- Choose the right words and speak efficiently, not speaking more than you have to.

- Measure your questions to comments ratio.

- Periodically monitor the time you spend speaking versus the time you spend listening.

- Work to create positive images with your words (for example, first reward what already has been accomplished, before discussing the long road ahead).

- Understand and explain situations as they are, and present them in a simple and understandable fashion.

Shut-Up and Listen

The reality is most leaders spend less then half the time listening. This makes sense, right?

- Leaders are great public speakers.

- Management's job is to tell people what to do.

- You don't become a manager by listening; effective managers are assertive and aggressive.

- Listening is passive and complacent.

Actually, no . . . this isn't what the data shows. Quite the contrary, successful leaders are those who have established trust, which is critical in creating a successful business that people want to work for and with. You create trust by showing people you care, and to show that you care, you listen. If you don't listen to your team, they will not trust you and only complete the minimum to get by; they will also not support your ideas (because they had no input in them) and will silently be hoping for failure.

There is a time to share your ideas and a time to value other's ideas. Being busy is no excuse: not listening to customers and teammates can cost a lot more in the long run than whatever fire you're running off to fight. Working on the balance between speaking and listening is no easy task. Having worked in many countries, I believe the ability to listen can be affected by someone's upbringing and further influenced by national cultures, but for the most part it is a personal trait. A lot of poor listening can be traced back to your formative years; if during your early childhood, you were not listened to by adults, you will find it more difficult to posses good listening skills. It can also be affected by the company's culture, for example, how meetings are conducted. Even when people do listen, on average, we do not listen very well. An untrained listener will retain only about half of the conversation immediately afterward, and during the course of the next few days will forget about half of that again. The remaining twenty-five percent is what we are left with.[20] Yet managers are often promoted because they are noticed, and most feel that comes from talking instead of listening. Instead, consider a promotion coming from those who trust you, knowing that trust comes from the care and competency that are demonstrated by listening closely, and only then making insightful contributions.

To believe that speaking creates authority and that having the podium puts you in control is simply incorrect. Leading without power is where the true advantage comes from. When really listening to others, you understand how to best approach them and meet their needs, which then supports the organization's ultimate requirements. A good listener not only understands what someone is saying but also comprehends his or her feelings, and this results in people believing they have been heard.

Improving Your Listening

Whether or not you were listened to as a small child might influence you listening skills, but it is an acquired skill that can be improved throughout your life. To sincerely listen, you need to take into account that the average person speaks between 110–150 words/minute, while the average listener can process between 400–500 words/minute. This can be referred to as the speech-hearing gap, and it means you must recognize distractions and quickly refocus. Some days, distractions come easy; for example, a telephone's ringing, observing how someone is dressed or that his or her hair is dirty. Other days, you are more focused and you ensure the speaker feels he/she has been heard. The best ways to overcome taking mental holidays when listening are as follows:

- Use head nods and verbal affirmations to confirm you are following along.

- Paraphrase what has been said.

- Clarify when more information is required.

- If the vocabulary is unclear, ask for clarification.

- Summarize, especially when multiple members of the group have contributed.

Teammates will also follow a leader's example, so if you can get leaders to listen more, the organization will begin to follow the lead. Although it simply comes down to attitude and motivation, people hear what that want and block what they don't want to hear. Work to create the awareness that listening is the basis of trust, and that we like people we can trust; therefore, good listeners are better liked and get further in life.

Another consideration to improve your listening is not to multi-task. Some people say they can read and listen at the same time, but nothing can be further from the truth. Imagine the disrespect and lack of trust you create with the speaker if you are reading while he or she is speaking. Even the dictionary's definition for listening ("to make a conscious effort to hear") flies in the face of multi-tasking while listening. People need to feel they've been heard.

Toyota's meeting structure is another solution to improve listening. Most of the meetings I attended while working with Toyota were divided into two parts: first was a five or ten minute structured dissemination of information that pertained to everyone in the room.

During this period, issues were identified that needed to be resolved between a select few in the room; those with open issues were acknowledged to stay behind for the second part of the meeting and resolve those matters in small groups. This is quite different to meetings where everyone remains in the room for the duration, and while a few converse to resolve a problem, the others whom are not involved begin daydreaming or planning their weekend activities.

In your Cultural Transformation Plan, evaluate the listening ability of the leaders in the organization. This can be done through some awareness and self-assessing, along with feedback from teammates. Where you identify gaps with your desired cultural objectives, you need to make a plan to close the gap. Some of the ideas presented in this section may prove helpful, as well as seeking other solutions.

Nonverbal Signals May Transmit More

Nonverbal symbols frequently convey more meaning than the words you are speaking. Studies indicate that people believe body language more than the words someone is using. If a leader's behavior or actions do not match his or her words, people believe the leaders really do not care about them. It is easy to tell from a combination of verbals and nonverbals whether the culture is positive and full of energy or negative and struggling to survive.

The actions that transmit nonverbal meanings can be divided into four groups:

- Body language

- Eye contact

- Tone of their voice

- Facial expressions

If body language is friendly, open, or shows concern, teammates are more receptive and open to listening. Effective eye contact also shows concern for the team and increases the effort of listening and understanding. Think of the various tones of voice your spouse utilizes and the different meanings they carry; that easily translates into the work place when the team leader enters with anger or stress in her voice, we are mentally prepared to decide how open and hard we will listen. As an example, think how many ways you can convey the phase "We need to talk." Through your choice of words and the tone of your voice, a lot of different meanings can be expressed that trigger one form or another of how we are going to listen. Facial expressions are very obvious: if you smile, look alive, and look interested, your communication will be more successfully received. Appearing very serious does not necessarily increase someone's importance; a smile relieves tension that opens people to being more receptive listeners.

Just as actions carry meaning so does a lack of action or bad habits. Being late or having a sloppy personal appearance affects how the team may interpret the words being used. Most of us who are timely associate waiting as a sign of disrespect, meaning someone else's time is more important than our own (one idea I have seen is a slush fund jar where anyone late puts in $1). Other missing actions may be forgetting to make a quick welcome or recognition for those who have taken time to come and participate in a meeting. Sometimes the little things add up.

Nonverbal communication in your leadership is one more area of awareness that should be evaluated against the new culture you are trying to create to support your strategic objectives. It may appear you are considering a lot of inconsequential items in creating the Cultural Transformation Plan, but organizational culture is not tangible and, therefore, hard to define because it is the sum of a lot of behaviors and traits. These can be reviewed in isolation but must be combined into a plan to have an impact on the culture.

A combination of awareness, self-assessment, and feedback from colleagues should help in evaluating who needs to consider changing, and which nonverbal signals they need to improve. You can start by evaluating the current status of the leadership in terms of how well they communicate.

Coaching and Mentoring

If the word coach conjures up someone on the football field blowing his whistle and yelling, this section will change your mindset. By "coaching," I am referring to engaging the hearts and minds of your team in reaching the organization's as well as their personal goals by encouraging everyone to do the proper thinking.

Coaching is quite a change from the traditional notion of using a pre-determined management plan to implement and control the strategy. Present-day with the rapidly changing environments in which we find ourselves, leaders cannot assume they can control the details of what goes on; instead decision-making must be delegated to allow plans to continuously be adapted (this requires thinking to take place at all levels in the organization). In these times, the role of leadership has changed to developing the team to understand how they can act independently to support the strategic goals; in other words, you need coaches—not managers—to lead the implementation of a deployed strategy.

Coaching is the best way to develop and engage the team, although those professional and technical people who have succeeded based on applying their own skills, or from working independently now have their success being based on a team outcome, they must contend with a level of emotional intelligence that is likely to make them uncomfortable coaching someone (they've always done the thinking and instead they need to encourage others to think about the *right* things). Coaching is not something you can do to someone; that person has to mentally grant you permission to be his or her coach, it must come in the form of a pull not a push.

To be a coach, you must first understand who you are, how you're perceived, and what are your strengths and weakness; that is why recent feedback or self-assessment questionnaires are the first steps toward improving your coaching.

Utilizing coaching requires many of the previously discussed cultural transformation steps as prerequisites, including traits and behaviors in the self-assessments, using the right words, having courage, and humility and listening. If you are going to self-assess your own coaching ability include some of these questions:

- Do you mostly give answers or do you ask lots of questions?

- Do you give (or push) advice?

- Are you a good listener?

- Are you patient or always in a hurry?

- Do you avoid conflicts or manage them with the facts?

- Who leads problem solving?

- Do you value everyone as a human being?

- Do you go and see, and then ask hard and challenging questions?

- Do you focus on succession planning by trying to develop leadership skills in others?

- Do you see good relationships as a business asset and competitive advantage?

Let's try to define what coaching is. A coach needs to give direction without giving directions. A coach develops people, they do not teach or advise as that is pushing information on someone. You have to assume you don't know what's best for others, in my case it's challenging enough to know what's best for myself. Ideally you coach to develop, although at times it might be necessary to coach for correction. Quoting Fijio Cho, head of Toyota North America, the ideal coach:

- Gives him or her the job as their own.

- Let's them think, let's them try.

- Helps him/her to see.

- Forces reflection.

To be a leader, you must leave the meeting room and go see; you have to ask the hard and challenging questions encouraging team membership to refocus perspective. You are defining the situation and facilitating agreement/solutions so that they can feel ownership. You don't produce the answer; you provide a system or process for *discovering* the answer—or just the next steps. You are not only developing better leaders, you are also developing positive relationships. You also do not isolate yourself from the truth and are more likely to have more honest two-way discussions with your team, this nonjudgmental awareness will also allow you to identify opportunities to take up with your coach (as each coach is also to be mentored by a coach), so that it can work in both directions.

Your Cultural Transformation Plan needs to recognize that coaching also focuses on personal development, which should be connected with you objectives in succession planning. Every leader can develop his or her replacement as part of a succession plan, and coaching is the best format. Therefore, you need to have these objectives clear as we identify our coaching relationships, and identify the mentor and mentee's in the transformation plan.

Mistakes Resulting in Poor Coaching

A good way to identify actions to improve your coaching is by considering some of the typical mistakes made that result in poor coaching; in other words, identifying management traits that need to be resolved to become a leader.

- **Evaluating and identifying problems,** and then attempting to coach a remedy.

- **Keeping quiet until you have the data for a strong case.** This results in advising and giving direction; you want the mentee or team to be gathering the data and forming their own perspective.

- **Too busy to coach.** Make time; otherwise you will be taking decisions, which will not win over the hearts and minds of the team. Also, you are likely to wait until you have a long list of issues, instead of focusing on one or two and resolving those at their root cause.

- **Dominating the conversation or expressing anger.** Speak less than one minute at a time after reflecting on what you are going to say and selecting your words carefully; otherwise you are likely to preach and dominate. Anger will limit participation, making it personal and emotional instead of fact-based. Also don't be impatient for a solution, don't fill the silence, use it as a time to reflect about what you want to say or ask next.

- **Telling others the solution.** Although you might feel a certain level of intelligence and have a lot to offer, remember that they will not own it; your role is to facilitate

- **Not clarifying your interests.** Your leadership when coaching is connected with who you are as a person, and this should be clearly communicated.

- **Denying your faults or mistakes.** Be part of a learning organization by admitting faults and creating a two-way dialogue in this manner.

- **Assessing performance; watching/analyzing to assess what's wrong.** You need to express empathy and ask questions and let the person come to their own conclusions.

- **Identify strengths, don't focus on weakness.** In every situation you should first identify strengths before prompting questions and allowing the person to identify the weaknesses.

Remember that people don't naturally resist change, they resist *being changed.* When someone is in the center of their own learning, he is the process owner and is energized and in charge. He doesn't feel he is being changed.

Steps to Becoming a Better Coach

Coaching should be likened to your strategic plan. Every leader who participates in the strategic planning should have a coaching plan, including being a mentor and a mentee. (First, people need to be coached, and then they can become coaches.)

Of course, coaching might not have a clear top-down or bottom-up roll-out; it depends where you identify existing leadership and coaching skills. If your Cultural Transformation Plan has already identified individuals with more leadership skills, those same people should answer the previous questions about their coaching skills (or take a coaching self-assessment). If they appear to be your most qualified coaches at this point, identify who they could start coaching and how to structure the process, how to create accountability, how to ensure focus, and how to have the persistence to create the next generation of coaches.

Remember, that you need to be given permission to coach. You cannot force coaching on someone, so you need to evaluate each coaching relationship's potential for success. If you listen, are helping provide feedback, and are increasing someone's capacity as a leader, that person is likely to seek your assistance in reaching a conclusion. If it appears this partnership is not taking shape, try to understand why it is breaking down and work to resolve that before considering other partnerships. Many of these relationships develop on their own, when people find an intelligent and insightful listener who helps them grow professionally, and it evolves from there.

A few steps in moving your organizational leadership toward a coaching mentality are:

- Clearly define responsibilities for everyone on the team. Through self-awareness of your current leadership and coaching abilities, determine whether the plan for you is to first be a coach or to be coached. Who will coach whom?

- Consider hands-on coaching workshops to develop your coaching abilities.

- Develop a means to track and measure success. This can involve individual monitoring of: telling versus asking questions, how often you go and observe, it can also involve feedback from colleagues on how you are doing (who feeds back to whom should be identified in the Cultural Transformation Plan).

- Seek any standardization of routine that helps increase your level of coaching.

- Learn and share experiences from coaching.

Adding to the Cultural Transformation Plan

You want to add the awareness and tangible steps identified here to your Cultural Transformation Plan (continue building onto Steps 2 & 3, as shown in Figure 6.1), since a documented plan that defines actions and a PDCA loop has a better chance of success. You need to know the current state and what your targets are in terms of coaching. Focusing first on bad habits is easier then adding new behaviors; for example, if someone delivers bad news, instead of punishing the messenger, try first to thank them for delivering the information. Working on these behaviors can be better accomplished by identifying peers to help remind you when a bad habit expresses itself, and selecting which peers can help is something you can visualize in your Cultural Transformation Plan. Changing bad habits or remembering when new behaviors are appropriate is not easy to do in isolation, which is why the plan is developed and visualized together, as a leadership team. Naturally coaches should also help remind you of bad habits through questioning.

In the case of coaching, instead of using only self-assessments (best identified during the Awareness/Analysis step explained in Chapter 7), you might also consider group feedback assessments of how others perceive you (refer to Figure 7.1). Try not to evaluate, instead present perceptions in an open and constructive format. Often, an external coach facilitating the conversation can achieve the best results. This group feedback will also help in identifying among which parties a coaching relationship will work best.

So self-assess all of leaders' coaching abilities against your strategic and cultural objectives, and add the results in the Awareness/Analysis step and Planning cells (Steps 2 and 3 in Figure 6.1), as appropriate. Each leader in the Cultural Transformation Plan should be either: coaching (assuming have the necessary skills), acquiring or improving skills, or at least be working to determine who can coach them so that they have a role model.

Figure 9.2 summarizes what needs to be added into the Cultural Transformation Plan.

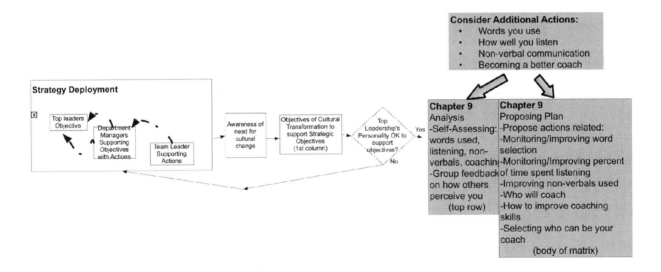

Figure 9.2 Process Steps through Chapter 9

Summary

It is easy to make people feel small, but it takes a real leader and coach to make people feel great in their professional lives, and this is significant in reaching your personal and organizational objectives. Those who are too busy and always fighting fires will never realize the benefits of focusing on the behavioral issues. Many of the soft skills we have discussed to this point are required in a leadership coach, so the Cultural Transformation Plan should be growing to include these actions, moving the entire leadership team toward becoming a team of coaches and continuing the personal growth throughout the organization that naturally results in a more successful company.

Understanding when intuitive thinking is dangerous to your decision-making, choosing the right words, communicating positively with nonverbals, and learning to listen are all behaviors that make a good coach. Leadership coaching helps both in personal development, succession planning, and meeting the organization's strategic objectives. A good coach is also likely to have most of the following traits or behaviors: good listener, patience, values everyone as a human being, unafraid to confront conflicts with structure and facts, facilitates but does not direct, goes and sees, asks hard and challenging questions, does not hide information, enjoys developing people, only teaches or advises when there is a pull from the team, does not know what is best for others, does not need to prove his or her intelligence, does not need to always get two cents in, accepts constructive feedback, does not deny his or her own faults, sees the value of coaching and makes available time, and focuses on positives and strengths instead of negatives and weaknesses. Usually coaches are also leaders, and leaders' traits can be summarized this way: great communicators and listeners, empathize with their teams, approachable, concerned with the teams development, and also lead by example.

In Chapter 10, we'll explore the theory behind learning organizations and evolve that into practical improvement steps to be considered for your Cultural Transformation Plan.

CHAPTER 10

Creating a Learning Environment

A *learning organization* is one in which members and teams continually acquire knowledge, and the sum of that learning is at a pace swift enough to prosper in their dynamic environments. Knowledge increases productivity and competitiveness as well as the goodwill of an organization, so learning—and transitioning that information into customer value—is core to your prosperity.

In today's uncertain global economy, more adults are continuing their education to stay ahead. The proportional increase of adult students (age 25 and older) has been greater than that of younger students. From 2000 to 2010, the enrollment of those under the age of 25 increased 34 percent, while those aged 25+ rose over 42 percent,[21] and the trend is expected to continue. This boost in adult learning must also continue inside your organization, and that is the focus of this chapter: how to best learn within a company.

Do Learning Organizations Exist?

The concept of a learning organization was popularized in the 1990s by Peter Senge's book *The Fifth Discipline*. During this period, a lot of training was performed, and some *Fortune* 500 companies appointed chief learning officers. Even so, it still remains difficult to find working examples of a learning organization, but in today's dynamically changing environments, creating an organization that can learn and stay ahead of the competition is likely more important than ever.

Although I cannot offer you a real-life example where it has been successfully implemented across the organization, I can begin with the theoretical concept of a *learning organization,* and then discuss specifically how the concept has been adapted to work successfully in individual and group learning. Understanding individual and group learning is the real value to your organization, and it is critical in sustaining your cultural transformation. Most of us manage and sell knowledge in one form or another; therefore, how we learn and acquire information are key concepts of our competitiveness.

What Can be Learned by Studying the Theory of a Learning Organization?

A learning organization is one that constantly aids the learning of its team members to continuously improve itself. This develops from external pressures to remain competitive and should evolve in support of the organization's strategy deployment. Naturally, you need to learn faster than your competitors, and this involves constantly employing learning and feedback loops. Strategy deployment must help to educate and connect all levels to the reality of the external environment and needs of the customer; the strategy deployment matrix discussed in Chapters 2 and 3 does just that. So, at this point, if we assume that you have deployed your strategy throughout the entire organization, and began working through your Cultural Transformation Plan, you should also have identified structural issues that encourage you to work toward a flatter organizational construction. This means you need only to determine which concepts from the learning organization can help you reach your objectives.

You know more learning (related to the organization's products or services) is always better than not learning, as learning increases the intellectual value and/or goodwill of an organization. Also key in your consideration is that learning is an individual activity based on some type of experience or training (although not necessarily formal or structured training). In fact, studies have shown that most learning does *not* come through formal training, but instead through on-the-job learning that comes from working in groups with colleagues. Experiences, discussions, stories, and reflection are some of the key elements that result in the most profound learning experiences within an organization. It is in these areas that you want to focus on and build from.

Do not confuse the fact that much of our knowledge begins its development informally, although some more formal training might be utilized to create the desire to continue this informal learning. In this instance, structured training is being used predominately for creating awareness (and whenever you decide teaching is the best option, look for hands-on workshops and simulations).

People learn most deeply through real-life situations, in which something depends on their increase in knowledge. At the same time, the speed and depth of knowledge is increased when this learning is shared within a group, because learning also has an emotional and social side. The most measurable improvements in knowledge have been documented to come from group learning through adaptation or some informal mechanism. With this in mind, encourage shop floor team members as well as transactional process leaders to create the type of environment that guides reflection and reporting back. Another factor that enhances learning is trust and security, which result in the psychological confidence to explore and make mistakes. If you cannot question and make mistakes, then the fear factor keeps you quiet and inhibits any gains in knowledge.

Keep in mind a few characteristics that foster an environment that supports social learning and leads to breakthrough objectives. Some of the areas that improve individual and group learning include:

- Shared vision (through strategy deployment)

- Open mentalities (by identifying and reducing individual, group, and organization bias)

- Individual commitment to learning (hiring and developing people who are not afraid of change and like to improve)

- Shared learning (improves speed of learning, by group sharing)

- Demonstrated trust (encourages participating and questioning)

- Providing people time and space to connect

As a company grows and becomes more structured, individual thinking can be impeded, which is why learning organizations are supported by flat organizational structures. Creating a proper problem-solving culture is also discouraged when a large organizational structure drives you toward more rigidly structured thinking, resulting in quick, single-loop problem resolution (defined in the following section), although it does not allow you to resolve the issue at its root cause. Problem solving and learning go hand-in-hand, and leadership must value these traits and be responsible to foster an environment where they thrive.

Steps to Foster a Leaning Environment

Let's take a pragmatic approach to creating an individual and group learning environment, based on hands-on experience. Any approach you utilize requires you to identify shortfalls in knowledge and skills, and determine whether these shortfalls can be developed internally or must be acquired externally. Let's take a look at how to proceed, assuming you feel the skills can be developed internally.

Recognize and Reward Learning

Focus on encouraging individual learning and openly recognizing such learning. Encourage new knowledge to be shared with the group and even documented as the organization's intellectual property. Center your efforts on those who want to grow (which pulls along those less motivated). In the hiring process, Human Resources should utilize all available screening techniques to weed out individuals not interested in personal learning and growth (that is, those with a closed mindset). Identifying those with a closed mindset may be accomplished through the use of online pre-employment tests (personality assessments), as discussed in Chapter 7. A learning organization is often described to be a sum of individual knowledge, so weed out those without an interest in learning.

Recognize and Discard Biases

Leadership should become experienced in distinguishing all types of biases. Such biases are part of the memory of the individual and the organization and form the basis for certain behaviors, norms, and values. An open culture (with the trust and confidence to question) can be created by moving toward *triple-loop learning*:

- **Single-loop learning:** When small changes are required and implementing a procedure or solution resolves the problem, you go through the loop one time and move to the next problem. An example could be raising the price on a non-profitable product or service.

- **Double-loop learning:** After implementing a solution, you enter the second loop by considering your actions against your assumptions or hypothesis and try to gain insight about why a particular solution worked.

- **Triple-loop learning:** After implementing a solution, and then considering your actions versus your hypothesis (second loop), you enter a third loop by looking deeply into how the problems and solutions are related; this should help in understanding and changing your bias or point of view. You want to better understand why you made a choice, and how your previous actions led you to your current problem.

Deploy Long- and Short-Term Objectives

For individuals and groups to focus their learning on what is important to the company's success, they need to have the same vision, which involves understanding both the market and competitors. This means updating and communicating your market analysis frequently to team members. Properly deploying your strategy (as discussed in Chapters 2 and 3), will direct the team's learning toward a common vision.

Encourage open Dialogue and Discussion

Because most learning is informal and at the individual and group levels, members need the confidence to make mistakes and share what has been learned. In larger organizations, this might involve *knowledge management;* that is, generating, gathering ,and sharing knowledge, if not in person then through an inter-company digital/social sharing site. Accepting change is easier after questioning and discussing it.

Put Feedback Analysis into Place

For any key decision you make, write down the expected results. Weeks or months later, compare your expectations to the actual results and see what can be learned about your strengths. Doing so allows you to build on your strengths and avoid areas of weakness. Such analysis can also be implemented on a more systematic basis by organizing regular feedback loops for critical processes. For example, I continually encounter sales forecasts that are rarely compared to actual sales results, but doing so leads to discussions and brainstorming of how to improve.

Today's Workplace Learning

Contemporary workplace learning can take various forms, including standard work/job training, company documentation or other sources (online and off), meetings and conversations, e-learning, classes and workshops, professional association conferences, and external networks. Depending on your market and the speed of change, leadership should recognize which type of learning holds the best value and help in gaining knowledge that supports the company's vision, and then those formats should be optimized and promoted.

This chapter gives you a few items to add to your Cultural Transformation Plan:

- Reviewing organizational structure to ensure work tasks and processes incorporate learning loops

- Increase dialogue where questioning is encouraged, helping avoid teams turning to mob mentality thinking because no other information was available

The dialogue you want to create involves two or more people questioning each other, and this means questioning each other's beliefs and assumptions. Leadership must educate their teams that such discussions are not about winning the argument, but about advancing understanding, reflecting, and learning. Dialogue leads to valuable organizational knowledge when it attempts to answer questions aligned to the company's vision, without questioning the company vision itself. Therefore, you want to encourage reducing biases and suspending assumptions to question everything *except* the company's vision and objectives, as this would be counterproductive.

Accepting That Criticism Is Part of Learning

An organization must accept that nobody is perfect and things will go wrong. With this realization, you can put in place systems to learn from mistakes. While working with Toyota, when a problem was encountered I always admired how they did not point a finger at an individual, instead they tried to understand the root causes and how they could make the process more robust, preventing this mistake from reoccurring. A metaphor for Toyota's thinking is, if you start pointing a finger, three fingers are always pointing back at you, which indicates that you should question what policies or procedures the organization can put in place to avoid repeating this, before looking for a scapegoat.

Some suggestions in accepting criticism are as follows:

- Listen carefully and objectively, and then consider which parts of the critique you are inclined to agree with. Try not to get defensive, as objectivity and learning will be lost.

- Listen carefully, and then analyze and evaluate. If you've heard this feedback before from various people, it should hold more weight. Ask what you could do to correct it.

- Discuss criticism openly; do not walk away and let anger build or hold a grudge, as there is no value in that. Once you stop listening, there is no chance you will ever agree with a critique and, hence, no possibility for improvement.

Obstacles to Learning

Becoming a successful learning organization, means learning from past mistakes; therefore, it is worthwhile to review where others have missed opportunities to increase their organizational knowledge.

- **Not empowering team members:** You need to empower people to learn and grow in line with their professional and personal ambitions. (Remember, however, that if you detect interest in gaining knowledge that appears to hold a hidden agenda or is for career growth outside the organization, this should not be financed by the organization.)

- **Threatened by change:** We all know people who feel this way and want the future to reflect the past. We also know this is a quick death for any organization. You don't want to create an environment in which learning is done only by a few and viewed as a selective activity. This is why you want to encourage sharing new knowledge, as this motivates the team to take part in learning and drives you to hire only those not threatened by change. Documenting improvements, training others, conducting group reviews, recognizing best practices, and becoming more extroverted are all some of the ways people overcome being threatened by change.

- **Growth of your organization:** As your organization grows and exceeds a few hundred people, structures and procedures increase to a point that inhibits learning and sharing. Team members are encouraged to work in a more rigid set of parameters, and there is less encouragement and trust to experiment. Customer focus through value-stream management and customer-centered metrics can help avoid this. *Note: Value-stream management* is different than traditional departmental/functional (or siloed) management: a multi-discipline team is responsible for a customer(s) product flow from enquiry to delivery of the product or service.

Summary

Requesting that colleagues sit at their desks and learn via reading books is likely to be of little benefit. Instead, you need leadership to distinguish between technical and social learning and focus on creating an environment where the interaction and process of gaining knowledge (social learning) is recognized as the pathway to technical learning. Such learning comes about by making the team feel safe in openly sharing their ideas, which is why risk-taking should be encouraged. Criticism, too, needs to be embraced and evaluated for its learning potential. Job-related learning should be identified and prioritized based on the goals of the organization. Some people will feel threatened by change and, therefore, not open to learning (i.e. those aligned with responses 1 or 2 in the mindset questionnaire in Chapter 7), but by creating trust, encouraging sharing, and not making learning an elitist activity, some will feel less threatened and become contributors.

The larger the organization becomes, the more effort it requires to keep an open, trusting and non-restrictive environment in place, although customer focus and value-stream management will go a long way toward supporting learning. The hiring processes should help filter out those who fear change, while leadership ought to have the ability to recognize and eradicate biases. Becoming officially recognized as a learning organization is not important;

instead, creating an atmosphere in which competitiveness is increased by knowledge generation and sharing is where you want to be.

The benefits to the organization of continuous learning are multi-dimensional, they include:

- Better linking of knowledge to the needs of the customer

- Increasing competitiveness with rapid innovation

- Process improvements throughout the organization

- More people focused, which improves employee satisfaction

Truly measuring what has been learned is not something I have found practical, as real learning takes place on an individual basis, mostly outside of formal training. Although many organizations track formal training, doing so does not necessarily prove whether any valuable knowledge gain has taken place.

The additional steps to be added in your Cultural Transformation Plan are graphically displayed in Figure 10.1.

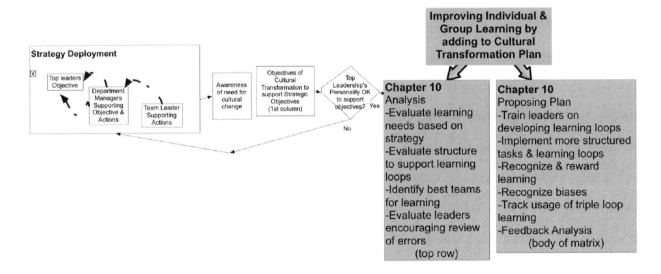

Figure 10.1 Process Steps through Chapter 10

Although everyone has their own style of following-up, some practical ideas will increase the success in sustaining the results; those are explored in the following chapter.

CHAPTER 11

Follow-up and Sustainment

Strategy deployment and the Cultural Transformation Plan require follow-up, although instead of being vague and only mentioning methods like PDCA (Plan, Do, Check, Act), let's spend a little time discussing what this means from a pragmatic perspective. The methodologies proposed in this book are continuous cycles that have no end, yet you can adopt some successful project management tools (*projects* being different from continuous cycles, because projects do have an end point) to help in adapting to the changing circumstances while trying to meet your objectives.

This follow-up translates to continuous reinforcement. The time necessary for this reinforcement will vary depending on the organization and person, although it must continue until the desire for the old ways (or old systems) are overcome by the benefits of the new system. Changing culture involves altering what is held between the ears, and this requires time, patience and reinforcement.

Levels of Follow-Up

Remember that there are various levels in which actions are assigned both in your strategic objectives and your Cultural Transformation Plan. For example, consider the high-level strategy-deployment matrix and the high-level Cultural Transformation Plan shown in Figures 2.1, 2.2, and 2.3 (see Chapter 2), with various levels of detailed implementation plans beneath these matrices that are not show here. These might include department, team, and individual activity plans that may take the form of a Gantt chart (a horizontal bar chart displaying a list of tasks to accomplish a plan, typically showing start and finish dates, as well as who is responsible).

Leader's Key Responsibility

In implementing an ongoing change, the leader(s) have many responsibilities in engaging and coaching the team, but it is critical to always maintain your focus on what you are trying to accomplish. What periodically happens after determining high-level objectives (the five or six most prominent objectives) is that each department, team, and/or individual begins working to detail the actions necessary to support the plan. Pet projects may be introduced or reintroduced at that point. During reviews, your leader must be vigilant that all effort being exerted focuses on reaching the objectives defined in the strategy deployment. If a person proposing an idea or task during this discussion cannot articulate how that idea or task will support strategic objectives, the leader should question whether that idea or task would be better placed at a lower priority or parked for a period of time. Some of these ideas that pop up are what I call *nice-to-haves,* and if time permits they might be alright to pursue, but doing so can quickly move you in the direction of *machine gun* or *kamikaze kaizen* (erratic continuous improvement), and this will deplete your limited resources.

One practical way to help in avoiding *kamikaze kaizen* is using Gantt charts (action lists), which include a column for the particular metric (or leading indicator) that will be improved by this task. If you have difficulty linking the task to the related measurement, then it should either drop off the list or be considered at a later point.

How to Define Actions at Any Level

The leader is responsible for getting things done; therefore, how you identify, motivate and communicate tasks is critical. Leaders should consider that the clearer and more concrete an action is, the less conflict you will experience in trying to complete it. Complicated or vague actions will likely be left as a last priority. Actions are continuously identified during the course of planning, reviewing, and realigning any plan or project. When defining actions for the organization, department, team or individual, consider the following:

- Start with a verb, for more clarity and motivation, for example: call, obtain, simulate, investigate, install, pilot, test, follow-up, document.

- During all discussions, try to summarize points with an action phrase (beginning with a verb), as this creates an action orientated culture.

- Be proactive (not reactive) when identifying actions; for example, create follow-up lists for yourself instead of reassigning responsibility for a task and erasing it off your list (and forgetting about it). Keeping it on your follow-up list will demonstrate the item's importance.

- Actions are identified all the time, not just in meetings; therefore, you need a method (including a medium) to capture and put them into a format that allows follow-up. Whether an idea pops into your head as you are driving home or taking a shower, you need to be able to document and communicate it.

- Actions need one owner to establish accountability. On any list or Gantt chart, designate a single champion or leader, not implying this person will do all the work but that he/she is responsible to oversee the task's completion. When facilitating teams, I often find they have a level of comfort putting down everyone's name that is likely to be involved in a task, but this leads to lost time in following up and frequently the shunning of responsibility (also known as "Teflon shoulders," because nothing sticks!).

There are also many types of actions to consider, although all should be documented in your plan. A few key types that should be handled differently are:

- **Delegated** actions should have the leader/manager's name designated as the champion, and his or her responsibility becomes to ensure that the task is completed.

- **Make-sure** actions are separate points to remind you to follow-up and confirm something has been completed, although it needs to appear as a written task, not just mentally noted in your head. The more public a plan, the more likely there will be follow through.

- **Awaiting** actions usually involve waiting for someone else to complete something. This is similar to a make-sure action in that you need to document it instead of relying on memory.

Every team offers a range, from very action-orientated people and to those who are unlikely to take on tasks. You want to create a culture where noting actions on paper becomes second nature. At the end of any meeting or discussion, ask everyone what they have captured on their to-do lists and identify missed or duplicated tasks.

Leading Various Personalities

When planning and reviewing, ensure that you are leading with positive energy and communicating the need for the changes and actions. A plan's importance might seem apparent or intuitive to you, but it might not resonate with all stakeholders, especially low visibility plans and projects. You also need to consider personal styles: for example, which members are self-starters and need little direction, and which require specifics? You must enable the team to get it done, and sometimes this will require translation into specific tasks for certain individuals, while for others, this type of detail may be insulting because they require only general direction. In either case, it is the leader's responsibility to understand what actions each person is planning to undertake and to regularly communicate progress and success.

You also need to balance personal contact (such as review meetings) with email and automated communications. Utilizing only personal contact can be exhausting, while following up by email is too impersonal. With email, you lose the benefits of team cooperation, body language, two-way feedback, and the like. During discussions, leaders can give the team recognition, and assume blame when appropriate. Handling of conflicts was also previously discussed as a skill leaders should poses, this is especially important during reviews. You need to decide the appropriate level and balance between email and face-to-face contact.

Steps to Consider for Follow-Up

Strategy deployment and your Cultural Transformation Plan are *not* to be viewed as projects (that is, having a beginning and an end) but some of the following project-management techniques might be useful:

- **Critical-path analysis:** This approach uses flow diagrams to visualize a plan and look for interdependent factors that are scheduled to overlap. I have rarely found critical-path analysis necessary, although an example that periodically manifests itself is when one or both of the CEO's two critical personality traits (agreeableness and/or emotional instability) do not align themselves with what is desired in the new culture (refer to Chapter 7), as these are difficult for anyone else in the organization to change. As these cause-and-effect elements are typically identified in a critical-path analysis, you would likely determine that, if a solution cannot be found, there is an effect that changes certain parts of the plan.

- **Gantt charts (also commonly known as action plans):** These are for scheduling tasks with beginning and end times, determining responsibilities, tracking/reporting progress, and doing budgeting. Commonly developed in Excel and in project-management software, they are used throughout various levels of an organization. The risk is that they do not show any interrelationships and have the danger of becoming tasks that do not lead to obtaining the strategic objectives. *Note:* As previously discussed, when I develop a Gantt chart with a team I usually add a column to describe which metric or leading indicator will be effected by the action. If the team cannot determine exactly how it will help, the task is a *nice-to-have* but not a priority and usually drops off the list.

- **Clearly defined actions that are delegated with SMART objectives:** SMART objectives are Specific, Measurable, Achievable, Realistic, and Time-bound. Consider each member's style and planning abilities, and treat them accordingly when specifying actions.

- **Contingency planning:** Planning and anticipating the unforeseen or recognizing problems will occur is an important part in any plan. Three areas where flexibility should be considered are related to timing, the level of required activity, and available resources.

- **Leaders gradually reduce the amount of direction provided:** Both strategy deployment and your Cultural Transformation Plan require more guidance and direction early on; this may be reduced as the team settles into their respective roles. A leader should not tell someone what to do but instead use leadership and coaching techniques to ensure buy-in and ownership. Early on, however, you might need to push until the team's clarity of purpose is more refined and roles and responsibilities are accepted among the team. At a later stage, the leader will only facilitate and enable (that is, coach) team members.

Follow-Up is the Leader's Responsibility

Motivating, updating, encouraging, facilitating, and enabling are all part of the leader's responsibilities during his or her follow-up. Various levels of freedom will be required for the various team members involved, of course: depending on their experience, creativeness, their own personality and behaviors, the leader must determine the regularity and appropriate level of follow-up. You need to focus on the results and also review the process utilized in achieving them.

Striking the right balance between face-to-face meetings and written communication is critical and will depend on the tasks and the personality of the team. Keeping team members happy and focused is the leader's goal, while recognizing that plans must be flexible and adjusted when required.

Reflecting and creating a learning cycle throughout the plan are also part of the leader's roles and responsibilities. Ensuring everyone understands what happened and why—especially when failures or mistakes take place—is critical. This must be done without naming and shaming anyone; it should always be viewed as a learning opportunity, thereby creating a learning organization. When reviewing situations, base them on facts (the data) to minimize emotional situations.

Consider company politics and how the effects from changes will be received by the team. Also be sure the concerns of the stakeholders (external to the working team) and the customer's needs are always at the forefront as the leader coaches the team.

Everyone wants to feel valued and remembered; the leader cannot allow busy schedules to result in his or her overlooking the human needs of the team. Leaders must make everyone feel special and valued, with recognition given to the team not to the leader as an individual. Leaders encourage questioning and debating, and are also the first to admit their mistakes. If a leader cannot find the time to perform these vital responsibilities, he or she should track how time is spent (by keeping a diary in 15-minute time increments for three weeks), and then examine whether the results are in line with their values and priorities.

Do not postpone giving feedback during any review session. The fear that criticism might demoralize the team or the desire to avoid confrontation will only compound the problem. Dumping all your bottled-up feedback during formal performance reviews makes members more resentful, as they are unlikely to recall the occasion when this transpired. Fact-based feedback discussed in a timely manner is more accepted and can create excellent two-directional feedback loops.

Visualizing Real-time Status of Strategy Deployment and Cultural Transformation Plan Matrices

The purpose of a visual review format is to highlight abnormalities, and this can be accomplished by marking actions either red, yellow, or green in the strategy deployment or Cultural Transformation matrices to indicate their current status. Doing so supports time management during reviews, as the focus can move toward resolving the abnormalities while recognizing those accomplished on schedule. Opponents of utilizing red/yellow/green indicate this color-coding only entertains those involved, but takes away from completing the activities. I disagree and find that, if properly utilized (for example, five minutes prior to a review, those responsible take highlighters and begin marking red to indicate the objective will not be met on-time [red], are slipping from target [yellow], or are on track or complete [green]), the team's discussion is more focused on problem resolution instead of trying to discern the status. Leaders should always focus in a proactive and positive way to remove road-blocks, while not forgetting to give credit for a job well done (remembering also to recognize the green highlighted tasks that are completed). The red/yellow/green shortens the duration of the meeting, as only abnormalities require discussion and a plan. Completed actions should be removed, encouraging next steps to be taken.

Summary

Although there is no standardized process or flow chart for following up, and each organization will manage it differently, depending on leadership style and traditions, the responsibility falls on the leader. Utilizing certain project-management techniques results in more productive and motivated reviews. Utilizing leadership and coaching techniques are about the best ways to review and follow-up. Specifically, capture all actions that support the company's goals and are discussed either during meetings or that pop-up during the course of the day. These ideas should be captured in a format that starts with a verb and includes a single champion for each task, as well as identifying which metric will be improved through this action.

CHAPTER 12

Conclusions

So it's simple, right? All you require are the majority of your managers functioning as leaders and your team's mentality aligned with a well-conceived strategy. The problem is, the odds of achieving this in the short term without a great plan or a lot of luck are similar to winning the lottery. Returning to the earlier definition of success = ability + luck, you are working to improve your abilities, utilizing a proven methodology to reshape some traits and behaviors that help in reaching both your continuous improvement and breakthrough objectives.

Certain societies and individuals display either more or less agreeableness publically, but whether they truly accept and support an idea remains to be seen. Corporate culture also plays a part in falsely nodding agreement, depending on how open their customs are to debating various ideas, versus being a company man or woman (a "yes man"). So short of a crisis or an overthrow of top leadership, what you want to build into your people is first a comprehension of why change is necessary, and then the required capabilities (including humility and courage). Remember, it's not just you that believes it's always the *other guy* that needs to change his traits and behaviors, the *other guy* views his attributes as ideal and believes it is the *other guy*, this is why non-biased self-awareness is a crucial focus. Following this, you must demonstrate leadership traits so team members evolve as leaders. Finally, you obtain their commitment through participation.

Anyone can change his or her mentality, but a new mindset cannot be forced. It requires awareness, motivation, dedication, and (most importantly) openness to learn and to accept challenges. Although it is difficult to *stop* doing something that has been part of your behavior, especially if you feel that it has contributed to your success, it is more difficult to *start* doing something that feels uncomfortable, threatening, or challenging, if you are not in an environment that supports experimentation or that accepts mistakes as part of the learning curve. The only other option regarding improvement is to do nothing, although real success is rarely based on continually repeating past behaviors that are not bringing the results you want. Improving culture can be synonymous with improving stability, which is important for all successful organizations.

Summarizing the Mechanics of Change

A brief summary of the major steps (in sequential order) is provided for you to confirm your understanding of what has been presented in this book. Although you might have various forms of some elements in place, you should consider if they meet the criteria set forth in this text. For example, experience has shown that many organizations believe they have some form of strategy deployment in place and a plan to improve their human assets, but if they do, it is rarely well communicated and bought into, as proven by asking random members of the organization what the corporate strategy is.

- Start with strategy deployment, in which leadership communicates to the entire organization the necessity of change and how the top-level objectives evolved. This is followed by dialogue of how each department can control or influence these points and summarized in a matrix to ensure that each potential link between an objective and various departments is examined and reviewed. Strategy deployment is not only *what* needs to be done in support of the customer, but also *how* you are going to accomplish it.

- Examine the current organizational culture (that is, traits and behaviors) in relation to either supporting or not supporting strategic objectives.

- Define traits and behaviors necessary to support both continuous improvement and breakthrough objectives at the organizational level if feasible.

- Define desired behaviors for each strategic objective at the value steam and departmental level.

- Create awareness of existing mentalities by involving all the ideas and self-assessments introduced and which the individuals have determined applicable, and note the differences between the current state and the desired traits and behaviors in the Cultural Transformation Plan.

- Review decision-making (intuitive versus analytical) styles and compare to desired traits and behaviors, identifying differences and actions in the Cultural Transformation Plan.

- Examine current management behaviors in the following areas:

  o Using the right language, words, and nonverbals

  o Leaders listening effectively and empathizing

  o Coaching and mentoring

- Identify actions necessary to create a learning environment and incorporate into your Cultural Transformation Plan.

- Continually review and revise (as necessary) both strategy deployment and your Cultural Transformation Plan.

The Gist of Dealing with Soft Issues

It may appear that a lot of inconsequential items are being considered when creating the Cultural Transformation Plan, but organizational culture is not tangible and is, therefore, hard to define, as it is the sum of many of behaviors and traits. Breakthrough objectives are rarely recognized without a clear, well-scoped strategy and some changes in organizational mentality, as demonstrated by many of the market leaders. Those who have had the privilege of visiting some leading companies within their industries often note a very different and dynamic frame of mind, one that is continually adapting to changes in the external environment and industry studies have confirmed this leads to higher operating margins. Therefore, the process discussed in this book is a continuous loop. It is not easy to stay ahead, as attested to by data indicating that less than one half of one percent[22] of U.S. companies stay in business for 100 years or more.

Poorly run companies with inefficient processes affect the morale of the team, so process improvement must be targeted to complement your strategy. Bad habits lead to waste, which causes dysfunction, poor motivation, and stagnated personal development. Strategy deployment is a key step in developing both a participative and results-driven culture.

A lot was discussed in this book about management versus leadership; I discuss where leadership should be focused outside the day-to-day firefighting. The higher you are in the organization, the more time you should be dedicating to strategy deployment and your Cultural Transformation Plan. Ideally, you want to transition to a point where the activities you identify as longer term objectives become incorporated into day-to-day routines. Building your Cultural Transformation Plan is required to create momentum and to help overcome barriers to resistance. That plan will create the velocity, although down the line your cultural change may become more self sustaining, and the format of your Cultural Transformation Plan will likely have to change to accommodate (possibly becoming less robust or formal).

You cannot send various leaders to random forms of leadership training and expect anything more than haphazard pockets of success. Instead, you need an overall plan that links soft leadership issues to tangible strategic objectives; that link is the critical connection between your strategy-deployment matrix and your Cultural Transformation Plan. For any particular department or individual, you should be able to look across their corresponding row in the matrices (see Figure 6.2) and understand where they have either control or influence and what improvements they are committed to.

These behavioral improvements can be better accomplished by identifying peers to help remind you when a bad habit expresses itself: use your Cultural Transformation Plan to select which peers to press into service. Changing bad habits or remembering when a new behavior is appropriate is hard to do in isolation; this is why the plan is developed and visualized by the leadership team.

So you want a Cultural Transformation Plan that respects and engages your team, provides an environment where people can be successful, ensures that nobody is humiliated, and guarantees that mistakes are acknowledged and viewed as a learning opportunity.

ROI (return on investment) is the bottom line in everything you do, but you can't control profit, as it is a result of sales (or revenue) minus cost. You need to understand your control over revenue and cost so that you can improve your profit. The Cultural Transformation Plan based on your strategy should take into account the link among those soft issues that need changing, and should tell you how this can be turned profitable for the organization.

Its interesting to note that, over the years, as I have asked managers to keep diaries of their working days (that is, tracking costs), on average they found that only about five percent of their time was spent on what the customer would be willing to pay for. This awareness is an opportunity to increase your ROI.

Summarizing some of the bad habits you want to counteract in your new culture:

- Overwhelming desire to tell others something they don't know, especially when it is irrelevant or not in their best interest.

- Failing to give recognition or credit while taking credit you don't deserve.

- Withholding information.

- Emotion, including angry outbursts, punishing the messenger, playing favorites.

- Setting unrealistic targets because you don't have the time to be involved in the details. For example, a dysfunctional organizational culture can be created by pushing a zero-defects mentality; it assumes perfection and mistakes will not be tolerated. Instead, go to *gemba*, where the value is added, and truly observe before determining any targets.

- Creating "non-negotiable" goals.

- Leaders not walking the talk.

- Advising or suggesting, instead of coaching through questioning, showing, and developing.

- Not developing a team of problem solvers.

- Silo mentality, where people perceive their responsibility purely in relation to the activities they own. (Instead, they must see the linkage and effects throughout the organization.)

- Leaders not letting go of minute details, rather than allowing others the responsibility and input.

- Defensive when questioned (not trusting that the questioning is a learning opportunity).

- Not communicating the vision and priorities frequently.

The leaders within only a few of the organizations I have supported can simply and effectively articulate the current strategy. Randomly surveying others throughout these organizations revels a smaller number who can explain the company's objectives and how they can contribute. Not having everyone *culturally on plan* is an insurmountable loss in creating a successful enterprise.

APPENDIX A

Glossary

<u>Chapter 1</u>

5S (workplace organization): A workplace discipline to increase efficiency by having easy access to only what you need in the working area, it is accomplished through five steps beginning with S: sort, straighten, sweep/shine, standardize, and sustain.

A3 Problem Solving: A Toyota method to guide the mentoring and dialogue of resolving a problem based on containing all information on an 11×17 piece of paper (known internationally as A3 paper).

Andon: An audio and visual indicator of machine status or a method for an operator to communicate an abnormality and quickly signal the need for help.

culture: Learned assumptions that are shared within group, resulting in predicable behavior and having an influence on decision-making.

kanban: A visual signal utilized to indicate when replenishment is necessary; a material-management system developed by Toyota based on replenishing consumption not based on forecasted usage.

leading Indicators: Indicators limited to a single process and change well ahead of underlying trend (or measurement) and linked to a metric or measurement (which are typically more historic).

PDCA (plan-do-check-act): Four-step improvement or problem-solving loop, based on scientific methodologies (and following Deming's circle).

SME (small and medium enterprises): Companies whose employee count (and, perhaps, revenue) are contained within certain limits.

Takt time: Time available divided by the customer demand; based on the supplier's available time in that particular process, and the customer's demand during that same time period.

Chapter 2

catch-ball: Participative approach to achieve buy-in to decision-making, in which information and ideas go back and forth, allowing in-depth understanding and development.

KPI (key performance indicators): Measurements or metrics that provide leadership with the most critical performance information for their area of responsibility. In this book, used interchangeably with metrics and measurements, but distinct from *leading indicators,* which are an early predictor linked to a metric.

Post-Its: Trademark for a slip of notepaper with an adhesive edge that allows it to be attached, removed, and easily revised, creating flexibility and encouraging input from all participants when brainstorming.

strategic decision: A choice that has significant consequences and places demands on resources.

Chapter 3

gemba: The real place where value is created (in manufacturing, for example, it is typically the factory floor).

Chapter 4

society's culture: Beliefs, behaviors, objects, and other characteristics common to the people of a geographic region (usually a country).

organizational culture: Beliefs, behaviors, and other characteristics common to an organization that affect decision-making and are responsible for creating the social and psychological environment.

Chapter 5

Cultural Transformation Plan: A developmental process to create self-awareness of leaderships' mindsets and compare those to the desired behaviors and traits that lead to reaching breakthrough objectives; this manifests itself in an action plan.

Chapter 6

CEO syndrome: An organization that operates according to the personality of either the CEO or the founder, but not in accordance with the organization's mission/objectives; this results in filtering information to that which agrees with the CEO's views.

Chapter 8

intuitive thinking: Thoughts and preferences that come to mind quickly and without much reflection.

analytical thinking: Systematic analysis that is logical, factual, critical, quantitative, and typically technical.

feedback analysis: Documenting your hypothesis when making a decision and, months later, comparing actual results to your hypothesis in attempt to improve you decision-making skills.

Chapter 10

single-loop learning (problem resolution): When small changes are required and implementing a simple procedure or solution resolves the problem.

double-loop learning (problem resolution): After implementing a solution, you enter the second loop by considering your actions against your assumptions or hypothesis, and try to gain insight about why a particular solution worked.

triple-loop learning (problem resolution): After implementing a solution, and then considering your actions versus your hypothesis (second loop), you enter the third loop by looking deeply into how problems and solutions are related; this should help in understanding and changing your biases or point of view.

Value-stream management: different from traditional departmental, functional, or siloed management, it is where a multi-discipline team is responsible for a customer(s) product flow from initial enquiry to delivery of the product or service.

Chapter 12

ROI (return on investment): a measurement that compares profits to the amount of capital invested, equal to net profit divided by net investment.

APPENDIX B

Strategy Deployment Example in an A3 Format

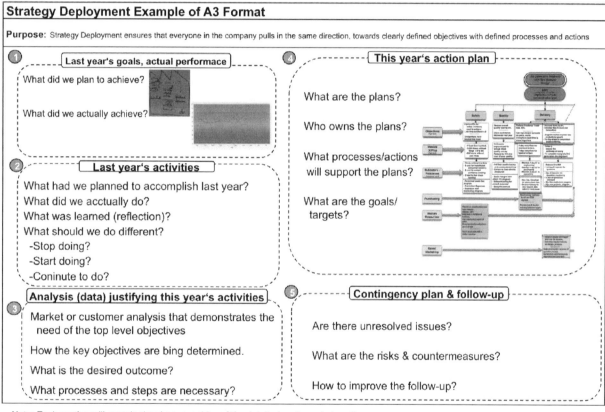

Strategy Deployment Example of A3 Format

Purpose: Strategy Deployment ensures that everyone in the company pulls in the same direction, towards clearly defined objectives with defined processes and actions

① Last year's goals, actual performace

What did we plan to achieve?

What did we actually achieve?

② Last year's activities

What had we planned to accomplish last year?

What did we acctually do?

What was learned (reflection)?

What should we do different?

- -Stop doing?
- -Start doing?
- -Coninute to do?

③ Analysis (data) justifying this year's activities

Market or customer analysis that demonstrates the need of the top level objectives

How the key objectives are bing determined.

What is the desired outcome?

What processes and steps are necessary?

④ This year's action plan

What are the plans?

Who owns the plans?

What processes/actions will support the plans?

What are the goals/ targets?

⑤ Contingency plan & follow-up

Are there unresolved issues?

What are the risks & countermeasures?

How to improve the follow-up?

Note: Each section will contain drawings, graphics of the details (as shown in box 1)

APPENDIX C

Team Leader Responsibilities

A team leader is an hourly paid person, generally promoted from within the team, who has the following responsibilities:

- Provide assistance to primary operator:

  o Answer Andon calls for assistance

  o Troubleshoot tooling problems

  o Determine when to call maintenance and who should respond (mech. or elec.)

  o Conduct changeovers

  o Execute pull systems

  o Handle defective material

  o Measure and track results

- Provide coverage for operator absenteeism

- Follow and procure material, when needed

- Complete overtime administration and record keeping (equalization books)

- Assist area supervisor to ensure proper rotation concepts

- Perform training and maintain training documentation (visual boards)

- Perform process monitoring (process and operator)

- Perform quality audits

- Provide input and monitor conformance to TPM procedures/schedules

- Provide input to root-cause analysis

- Provide documentation for machine problems/downtime causes

- Assist supervisor in ensuring proper scheduling of production

- Assist supervisor in ensuring timely and accurate completion of vacation schedules

- Assist supervisor in maintaining department supplies & indirect materials

APPENDIX D

OSKKK Methodology

OSKKK Methodology

1. Observation (for All Operations)
• Take the time to see what is happening in the work area by watching multiple cycles of the same process.
• Watch more than one person performing the process and note where standardization is lacking, especially when affecting quality or productivity.
• Document in writing the individual process steps in the sequence they occur.
• Identify the origins of variation in both the flow of information and the flow of materials.

2. Standardization (for Materials, Motions, Tasks, and Management)   defined as: the current optimized sequence of the process steps followed by team members that ensures quality, safety, and productivity.
• Prioritize where standardization is most critical to the organization, based on observations or data.
• Observe all team members' various methods for performing the task, and decide on the current standard (based on that which is best for quality, safety, and productivity).
• Have all members work to the current standard while discussing improvement ideas.
• Input 5S (workplace organization) to promote simplified and productive standardization to be put in place.
• Work to minimize/eliminate problems and interruptions to the process using problem-solving techniques.
• Ensure all flows and decision points in the process have a standard methodology.

3. Kaizen of Flow and Process (Information and Materials First)
(least costly to implement, $)

- Understand and map process flow (process mapping).

- Understand and map material flow (value-stream mapping).

- Improve flow of material and information to the work area.

- Identify all non-value add in both information and process flows, and then work to eliminate or minimize it.

- In businesses processes and material flows, work to reduce throughput time.

4. Kaizen of Equipment
(medium cost to implement, $$)

- Evaluate purchase of machinery or systems (i.e. software, automation, investment).

- Look at set-up time (SMED) and work to reduce it.

- Look to improve feeds & speeds (reduce machine cycles).

- Use OEE as the measurement to drive improvements.

- Understand operator workload in comparison to machine cycle times, eliminate forced waiting.

- Look for TPM improvements.

- Look to simplify machines.

5. Kaizen of Layout
(most costly to implement, $$$)

- Ensure previous steps of OSKKK have been worked on before rearranging layout.

- Collect data: process flows, capabilities, new products, bottlenecks, OEE, value stream maps, information flow, etc.

- Create a minimum of three layout proposals, with all showing flow arrows and complete correlation matrices.

- Ensure new layouts consider all lean principals and remove non-value added to justify costs.

- Work to improve the man-machine-materials ratio.

- Consider new machinery only after working to improve existing machines and incorporating all learnings into specifications for the new machine.

- Simulate the new layout either marking the floor (for existing layouts) or with cardboard mock-ups of the equipment (for new processes or products).

APPENDIX E

Simple Ropeloc Display of Data

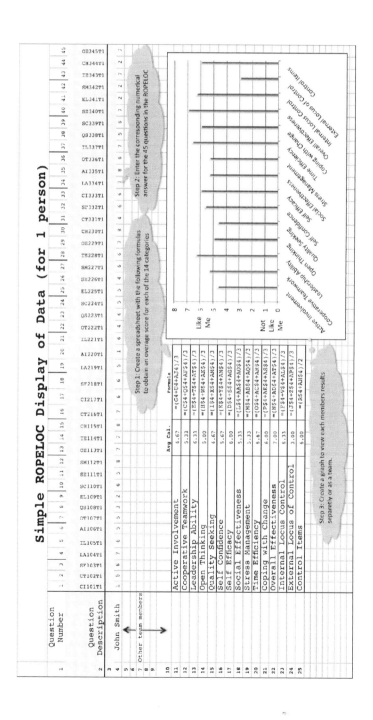

APPENDIX F

Training Within Industry Report: 1940–1945

	Percentage of Plants Reporting Results of 25 Percent and Over						
	May 1943	Sept. 1943	Feb. 1944	Nov. 1944	April 1945	July 1945	Sept. 1945
Production increased	37	30	62	76	64	63	86
Training time reduced	48	69	79	92	96	95	100
Manpower saved	11	39	47	73	84	74	88
Scrap loss reduced	11	11	53	20	61	66	55
Grievances reduced	(Not reported)		55	65	96	100	100

Source: War Production Board, Bureau of Training, Training Within Industry Service, September 1945, *The Training Within Industry Report: 1940-1945,* (Washington D.C.: U.S. Government Printing Office), p. 92.

ENDNOTES

[1] Casey, D. (2009). *The Role of Change Leadership in an Operations Excellence Transformation Model, CEO Surveys.* Lulu Books.

[2] Anginer, D., Fisher, K., Statman, M., (2008). *Stocks of Admired Companies and Despised Ones.*

[3] Huntzinger, J., (2002, volume 18, number 2). The Roots of Lean, *Target Magazine*, p 10.

[4] Jackson, T.J., (2006). *Hoshin Kanri for the Lean Enterprise: Developing Competitive Capabilities and Managing Profit.* New York, NY: Productivity Press.

[5] 2012, September. Staying Ahead, Executive Education, *Hemispheres Magazine*

[6] Culey, T. (2010). Building Cultural Acceptance Key to Lean Transformation. Retrieved from www.isixsigma.com.

[7] Gallop Poll (2012, Friday–Sunday, September 14–16). *The Wall Street Journal.* p. 29.

[8] "Mentality" defined, http://dictionary.die.net/mentality.

[9] Lane, G. (2007). *Made to Order Lean: Excelling in a High Mix, Low Volume Environment.* New York, NY: Productivity Press.

[10] Enron Scandal at a Glance (2002, August 22). *BBC News.*

[11] Goldsmith M., Reiter M. (2007). *What Got You Here Won't Get You There.* New York, NY: Hyperion.

[12] Schein, E.H. (1996). *Organizational Culture and Leadership,* Second Edition. Hoboken, NJ: Jossey-Bass.

[13] Giberson, T., Resick, C., Dickson, M., Mitchelson, J., Randall, K., And Clark, M. (2009, April 26). Leadership and Organizational Culture: Linking CEO Characteristics to Cultural Values. New York: Springer Science + Business Media. pp. 123–137.

[14] Walker, J., (2012, September 20). Do New Job Tests Foster Bias?. *Wall Street Journal*, p. B2.

[15] Roberts, B., Mroczek, D., (2008) Personality Change in Adulthood. National Institute of Health, Curr Dir Psychol Sci. February 1; 17(1): pp. 31–35.

[16] Brusman, M. Dr. Why Executives Thrive or Barely Survive, *Working Resources Newsletter.* Volume V, no. 12, pp. 1-2.

[17] en.wikipedia.org/wiki/Intuitive_thinking.

[18] Tetlock, P. (2005). *Expert Political Judgment: How Good Is It? How Can We Know?.* Princeton, NJ: Princeton University Press.

[19] Leemann, JE. (2002, April). Applying Interactive Planning at DuPont, *Systemic Practice and Research.* Vol. 15, No. 2.

[20] Atwater, E. (1992). *Adolescence,* Third Edition. Englewood Cliffs, NJ: Prentice Hall. pp 67–69.

[21] U.S. Department of Education, National Center for Education Statistics (2012). *Digest of Education Statistics.* NCES 2012–001, Ch 3.

[22] U.S. census data for 2006 lists the number of U.S. firms at 6,022,000; database of companies over 100 years old is now at 540.

[23] Manufacturing Performance Institute, 2011 Next Generation Manufacturing Study, 824 manufacturing surveys, National Executive Summary, 2011 MPI Group

[24] Towers Watson (2012), Towers Watson Global Workforce Study 2012, pp. 8

AUTHOR BIOGRAPHY

Greg Lane has owned and successfully transformed his own company, along with supporting others in leadership improvements in 32 countries, with diverse types of organizations. He has effectively led change while holding leadership and executive positions at General Motors and Delphi Automotive.

His 25 years of worldwide experience was strongly influenced while working for Toyota in the late 1980s, when he was one of a handful selected to be developed as a Toyota Key Person, through a year of specialized training in Japan. This included working with Toyota's top trainers, and then returning to train others within Toyota at their U.S. sites.

Greg learned early on that it's not technical tools and methodologies that drive the breakthroughs; instead, it's cascading leadership throughout the organization and focusing leaders on a clearly communicated and deployed strategy.

Today, Greg is internationally recognized as a coach in creating organizational change, and has been invited to speak on five continents about these successes. Also a recognized author, he has written the following books and published in leadership and technical medias:

- *Made to Order Lean—Excelling in a High-Mix, Low-Volume Environment* (Productivity Press, New York: 2007)

- *Mr. Lean Buys & Transforms a Manufacturing Company—The True Story of Profitably Growing an Organization with Lean Principals* (CRC Press, New York: 2010)

- Chapter 9 of *Toyota by Toyota—Reflections from the Inside Leaders on the Techniques That Revolutionized the Industry* (CRC Press, New York: 2012)

Greg is a facility member of the Lean Institutes in the USA and Spain, as well as lecturer of post-graduate lean studies at the University Polytechnic Barcelona. He holds a B.S. in mechanical engineering from the University of Wisconsin as well as an MBA degree with distinction from California State University. He speaks English, Spanish and German.

Greg and his associates provide very cost effective support at coaching successful cultural improvements and facilitating great leadership transformations. He can be contacted at glane@strategic-leaders.com or more information can be found at:
http://www.strategic-leaders.com.

Made in the USA
Lexington, KY
24 February 2015